Israeli Folk Narratives

Israeli Folk Narratives

Settlement, Immigration, Ethnicity

HAYA BAR-ITZHAK

Wayne State University Press
Detroit

09 08 07 06 05   5 4 3 2 1

Library of Congress Cataloging-in-Publication Data

Bar-Yitsḥaḳ, Ḥayah.
Israeli folk narratives : settlement, immigration, ethnicity / Haya Bar-Itzhak.
p. cm. — (Raphael Patai series in Jewish folklore and anthropology)
Includes bibliographical references and index.
ISBN 0-8143-3047-9 (pbk. : alk. paper)
1. Jews—Israel—Folklore. 2. Galilee (Israel)—Rural conditions—Folklore.
3. Kibbutzim—Folklore. 4. Israel—Emigration and immigration—Folklore.
5. Immigrants—Israel—Folklore. 6. Israel—Ethnic relations—Folklore. 7. Jews,
Moroccan—Israel—Folklore. 8. Legends—Israel. 9. Legends—Israel—History and
criticism. I. Title. II. Series.
GR285.B37 2005
398'.3295694—dc22
2005009204

The Israel Folktale Archives named in honor of Dov Noy (IFA)
permits the publication of all folktales included in this book.

∞ The paper used in this publication meets the minimum requirements of the
American National Standard for Information Sciences—Permanence of Paper
for Printed Library Materials, ANSI Z39.48-1984.

To the blessed memory of my dear friend
REBECCA SPITZ,
a lover of Jewish folklore

Contents

Preface ix

PART I.
THE SETTLEMENT IN THE LAND OF ISRAEL: KIBBUTZ LOCAL LEGENDS 1

1. "Forest of Thorns into a Flourishing Garden": Local Legends and Cultural Interpretation 7

2. Processes of Change in the Kibbutz as Reflected in Local Legends 29

PART II.
LEGENDS OF IMMIGRATION AND ABSORPTION 51

3. "The Camouflaged Plums": Sweet versus Bitter in Legends of Absorption of Polish Jews 57

4. The Legend of Yemenite Jews as an Expression of Immigration and Absorption 71

PART III.
ETHNIC FOLKLORE IN ISRAEL 91

5. Old Jewish Moroccan Women Relate in an Israeli Context 97

6. Ethnic Nonverbal Components in the Jewish Moroccan Saints' Legend 153

Notes 167
Bibliography 177
Index of Names and Places 185

Preface

This book brings together studies of the three main fields of Jewish folklore in Israel: rural settlement, immigration and absorption, and ethnic groups. Part 1 deals with stories about the initial settlement of kibbutzim. The period of Jewish national settlement in Eretz Israel in the modern age, an enterprise that in the words of the Balfour Declaration aimed at "the establishment in Palestine of a national home for the Jewish people," has been the subject of abundant historical and sociological research. The literary texts of the period have also been studied. Much less attention has been given, however, to its folklore. A number of important articles have been published in the periodical *Edot*, but they focus mainly on transcription and documentation. The most important reason for the paucity of scholarship in the field is the fact that folklore studies in Israel were initially gripped by a dilemma stemming from the traditional definition of folklore, which stressed antiquity. Rural-settlement folklore, by contrast, was the direct outcome of a revolution and—at least on the declarative level—the creation of a new world. Consequently, folklore studies tended to concentrate on Jewish ethnic communities that had immigrated en masse after independence and were seen as coming from a world in which there was a continuity of traditional patterns, a focus reinforced by the attractive exoticism of these traditions. But as the definition of folklore changed and settlement folklore aged, it too became the object of folklore research. Nevertheless, it should be emphasized that both folklorists and researchers in cultural studies preferred to concentrate on the "big" cultural narratives—what came to be designated as the myths of Israeli culture, such as Tel Hai and Joseph Trumpeldor, and the tower and stockade settlements (Katriel and Shenhar 1990; Zerubavel 1991; Gertz 1995).

In my studies of rural-settlement folklore I have focused on the periphery rather than on the center. My work concentrates on the legends that had practically no circulation in the country beyond the kibbutz community in which they crystallized and were retold. I have attempted to indicate the importance of these local legends for understanding and interpreting Israeli culture. An examination of the stories and the exposure of their symbolic dimension points to the complexity of the narrative of the local culture that these stories build, a complexity that expresses the ethos of Labor Zionism.

I conducted my studies during the 1990s. Accordingly, the storytellers tell the stories from a contemporary perspective that casts a critical eye on the past. Along with tales of the founders there are also stories told by the next generation. The developments that have transformed the kibbutz movement, which today stands at a crossroads, are also reflected here.

Part 2 deals with the folklore of the immigrants (*olim*) who reached Israel in the waves of mass immigration in the early years after independence. The folklore the immigrants brought with them from their countries of origin has received much attention, based on the traditional outlook of folklore studies as a "rescue operation." Later studies examined the changes in the immigrants' folklore subsequent to their encounter with Israeli culture (Hasan-Rokem 1982) and the emergence of local folklore in immigrant localities (Schely-Newman 1991). In my research into the immigration and absorption tales of Yemenite Jews, I scrutinized mainly the way in which the traditional sacred legend, which the Yemenite Jews chose to employ, reflects the new problems they had to grapple with in the Israeli context. In my study of the immigration and absorption stories of Polish Jews, I placed the accent on what Barbara Kirshenblatt-Gimblett called "culture shock and the creation of folklore" (1978). Unlike the Yemenite Jews, who chose to express the problems of immigration and absorption through the medium of the saints' legend, the Jews from Poland who came to Israel in the late 1950s employed realistic stories. This reflects, of course, the world of the beliefs and opinions of the different immigrant communities.

Polish Jews also told stories that express their traumatic meeting with Israeli society and indicate that folklore in the aftermath of traumatic contacts tries to express the trauma while providing a means for coming to grips with it. The immigrants' worldview, which my study uncovered, can provide an explanation for the mode of the stories' absorption in Israel. Thus, for example, the cultural outlook revealed by an analysis of the stories of Polish immigrants may help explain why this community is considered an "unproblematic" wave.

Part 3 deals with ethnic folklore. Even though immigration and absorption stories belong to the category of ethnic folklore, I thought it appropriate to make a distinction for two reasons: first, to emphasize the topic of immigration and absorption as standing on its own merits, and second, because in Israel today both ethnic folklore and a multicultural society are emerging many years after immigration to Israel, despite the attempt made in the 1950s to fuse immigrants into a national "melting pot" and provide them all with a uniform culture. Moreover, as Eyal Ben-Ari and Yoram Bilu have shown, immigrants are returning to patterns of ethnic culture in Israel many years after immigration and after they have acquired a degree of socioeconomic security. It is precisely the return to traditional patterns that provides the ethnic group with the tools needed to change their community from periphery into center. This has happened, for instance, in development towns, where the tomb of a holy man of the community, going back to the country of origin, has been "transferred" and as a result the town has become a pilgrimage center on the anniversary of the holy man's death, with everything this involves (Ben-Ari and Bilu 1981, 243–71).

We must take into account that the Jews' experience of ethnicity in Israel is different from what it was in the Diaspora. Rather than the ethnic identity of a religious minority in an ocean of non-Jews, in Israel they experience the ethnicity of Jews vis-à-vis other Jews. My studies address the ethnic folklore of Moroccan Jews in Israel, with an emphasis on the folktales created by elderly women. This folklore is typified, on the one hand, by patterns of continuity stretching back to their native country; on the other hand, though, it is influenced by the encounter with the Israeli milieu. My focus is on the wonder tale, the favorite genre of Moroccan immigrant women in Israel. I also examine the body language typical of narrators of the saints' legends of Moroccan Jews as it relates to the Israeli setting.

I take pleasure in thanking all those who assisted with the publication of this book, the Israel Folktale Archives, and the Saul O. Sidore Memorial Foundation for their generous grant. I would like to thank two of my students who contributed to my study of the stories of Gennosar: Rachel Duzzy, a teacher and educator at Kibbutz Gennosar, through whose work I first became aware of jujube stories, and Noa Shamir-Ronen, who helped me organize meetings with the storytellers and obtain material from the kibbutz archives.

This book is based on my studies that were published in the following journals: *Journal of American Folklore, Journal of Folklore Research, Jerusalem Studies in Jewish Folklore, Jewish Folklore and Ethnology Review, Contemporary Legend,* and *Cahiers de littérature orale,* and in the book *Oral Tradition and Hispanic Literature: Essays in Honor of Samuel G. Armistead,* edited by Michael M. Caspi. I would like to express my thanks to all of them.

This is my third book published by Wayne State University Press. Professor Dan Ben-Amos, the editor of the series; Dr. Arthur B. Evans, the former director; and Kathryn Wildfong, the acquiring editor, have made my association with the press a particularly happy one. I also thank Carrie Downes, the project editor, and Jill R. Hughes, the copyeditor, for their superb work. I owe a special debt of gratitude to my husband, Zeev Bar-Itzhak, for his encouragement and help.

I
THE SETTLEMENT IN THE LAND OF ISRAEL:
KIBBUTZ LOCAL LEGENDS

THE BIRTH OF THE STATE of Israel was preceded by a period of Jewish settlement based on a series of waves of immigration, or *ali yot*. The First Aliya, which began in 1882 and ran through 1903, brought an estimated twenty thousand to thirty thousand immigrants to the country. It was a direct outcome of the proto-Zionist Hibbat Ziyyon movement in Russia and Romania. The immigrants saw settlement of Eretz Israel—the Land of Israel—as a precondition for the revitalization of the Jewish people. It was during this period that the first Jewish agricultural settlements in the country were founded.

The Second Aliya (1904–14) comprised some thirty-five thousand to forty thousand immigrants. Most of them were members of various Zionist-socialist groups in Russia. Their decision to immigrate to Palestine was catalyzed by their disappointment with social reforms in Russia and the failure of the October 1905 revolution, which was followed by anti-Jewish pogroms. Even though this wave of immigration took place during a period of dual crises—in Eretz Israel and in the Zionist movement—it changed the sociodemographic structure of the Jewish community in Palestine (the *yishuv*), introduced new settlement patterns, and laid the foundation for the labor movement in Eretz Israel.

The Third Aliya (1919–23) brought about thirty-five thousand immigrants to the country. Preparations for the event began in the last year of World War I, in the wake of the Balfour Declaration. There was a preponderance of pioneering types—*halutzim*—in this wave, including many young people who had been trained by the *Hehalutz* organization in Europe. The principal achievement of the Third Aliya was the establishment of a number of agricultural settlements, both kibbutzim (communes) and moshavim (collective settlements where members work their own land but maintain certain services in common).

Another eighty-two thousand immigrants arrived in the Fourth Aliya (1924–31). Predominantly middle class, they tended to settle in the towns and cities, where they engaged in industry, trade, and crafts. The Fifth Aliya started in 1932, with around two hundred sixty thousand Jews coming to the country by 1944. Many were refugees from

Nazi Germany who arrived with capital assets that contributed to the development of industry, trade, and agriculture.

These waves of immigration were strongly future-oriented and focused on the establishment of a Jewish national home in Eretz Israel. The establishment of new settlements was the keystone of the Zionist ethos, and the period before the establishment of the state was called *Tequfat Ha'Yishuv* (the settlement period).

In the vision of the Zionist ideology, the social, occupational, cultural, and political functions of the future were imbued with a spirit of national identification, equality, and social justice. The central function and image that coalesced, from the time of the Second Aliya, was that of the *halutz*, or pioneer. There were variants on this image, but they all had a number of traits in common:

1. A readiness for self-sacrifice, manifested in making do with little and leading an ascetic life, in order to realize the national mission in the future: the *halutzim* were distinctly future-oriented and were accordingly willing to waive immediate rewards.
2. Manual labor in general, and agricultural labor in particular: these were perceived as a means to create a "new Jew" who would represent a departure from the exilic type.
3. The creation of a community that would lead to the evolution of a just society based on the spirit of utopian socialism.

During the Third Aliya the various ideological currents and kibbutz movements focused on the figure of the *halutz*. Membership in the movement and in a communal settlement was seen as the key element in the implementation of the ideology. The kibbutz was considered to be the classic expression of the *halutz* ethos and acquired an elite image as the embodiment of the central values of the age (Eisenstadt 1967, 13–15, 125–28).

The first kibbutz (Deganya) was founded in 1909 and was followed by a massive establishment of kibbutzim beginning in the 1920s. Establishing the kibbutz in the prestate period (*Yishuv*) was a voluntary act; its aim was the implementation of a clearly defined ideology that combined the Zionist-nationalist tenets postulating the establishment of a national home for the Jewish people in the Land of Israel with socialism aiming at the renewal of society and social justice in the spirit of utopian socialism and the vision of the Jewish Prophets.

As a young society operating on an ideological basis and under living conditions of extreme hardship, the kibbutz was marked by ideological rigidity. Despite the relatively small percentage of kibbutz members as compared with the total population of Israel, the kibbutzim had a central role and its members were regarded as social and cultural elite.

The kibbutz is, in great measure, the optimum laboratory for the generation of folklore (Gali 1989). It constitutes a large membership group—the kibbutz movement. Here, what links the members of the group is their ideology. A more limited membership group is the single kibbutz with all of its activities. Within the kibbutz there are smaller groups: the nuclear family, the extended family, groups of workers, and so forth. By its very nature, the communal way of life serves as a good breeding ground for the development of folklore. People constantly meet at their workplace, in the dining hall, and other locations, where opportunities arise for an exchange of experiences and the telling of stories. Some stories continue their lives orally, being transmitted on both intergeneration and intrageneration levels; other stories are written down, or serve as the background to the stories of various authors and writers.

However, only recently has folkloristic research been devoted to the kibbutz (Shenhar 1989), with the majority of kibbutz studies being sociological and quantitative (Shur 1972). The reason for this is apparently that folkloristic research in Israel has preferred to focus on the ethnic groups in Israel (Ben-Amos 1991, 43–45).

According to the vision of the founders, the kibbutz was supposed to be a model of life in a society that places the unification of the community in the center. It was a community that encompasses all areas of life. The shared areas of cooperation in the kibbutz were joint ownership of all means of production and consumption; joint organization of the work of production, services, and administration; and joint responsibility for the material and spiritual needs of the kibbutz members. All kibbutz children were educated together in the community's educational establishments; the kibbutz strived to consolidate a common worldview adhered to by all. All members were expected to contribute, by their work, each in accordance with his ability and qualifications, while the kibbutz, in turn, had to supply the material and spiritual needs of the members.

As early as the 1960s the kibbutz began to undergo a process of change out of necessity to adjust to a shifting Israeli reality. This process was first expressed in economic matters, such as the transition from agriculture to industry, as well as in the debate about hiring outside workers for the kibbutz. However, changes also occurred in matters concerning attitudes about the relationship between individual and group, which became even more strained with changing times and generations. Today the kibbutz largely finds itself at a crossroads as a result of far-reaching changes and conflicting orientations within the kibbutz society.

Many kibbutzim are going through a period of "privatization." The children's houses have been abolished on all kibbutzim; in many, the members' dining room has been closed, too. The once-reviled family unit has regained its dominance.

In what follows I will consider kibbutz local legends that are also legends of origin about the founding and early days of the settlement.

1

"Forest of Thorns into a Flourishing Garden": Local Legends and Cultural Interpretation

This chapter examines stories about the founding of Kibbutz Gennosar. As Tamar Katriel and Aliza Shenhar note: "Acts of settlement and the rhetoric of place attending them have been at the heart of Israel's nation-building ethos. The dense, at times uneasy, narrative symbolism in which past and present Israeli discourses of settlement have been cast became a shaping force in the communicative construction of the Israeli national sense from the very first Zionist efforts to settle the land at the end of the nineteenth century" (1990, 359). In their article, Katriel and Shenhar examine stories associated with the tower and stockade settlements that were central to prestate Israeli society between 1936 and 1939. These stories form a great national narrative that is told and retold in Israel and that "is one of the key scenarios in Israeli collective life" (376). By contrast, my study focuses on local legends of Kibbutz Gennosar that never circulated beyond its borders. As we shall see, these legends express the Zionist-socialist ethos and its accompanying problems.

Kibbutz Gennosar, which lies on the western shore of the Sea of Galilee, was started by a group of teenagers who were born or raised in Palestine and attended the Workers' Children School in Tel Aviv. Most of them continued their secondary studies at the Ben-Shemen Youth Village, where, augmented by classmates, they formed a settlement core group. In the 1930s most settlement core groups were composed of immigrants affiliated with one of the pioneering movements. Forming a group meant that its members lived in a temporary camp while supporting themselves with wage labor in anticipation of establishing a permanent settlement. This group followed the same pattern.

Its members received agricultural training in the established communal settlements of Deganya and Kinneret, on the Sea of Galilee. In 1934 the group moved to Migdal, a freeholder's village a few kilometers from present-day Gennosar, and settled into a vacated camp that belonged to the Jewish Agency. The group became known as the Youth Group in Migdal. In 1936 it was joined by a group affiliated with the Noar Haoved movement, whose members hailed from Ein Harod, Givat Brenner, and Tel Yosef. Groups began settling in the Gennosar Valley in 1937 under unusual circumstances, including their staking a claim to a plot of land and a confrontation with the settlement institutions. Even today, some veterans of the affair refer to it as an incident that is better passed over in silence. Others acknowledge that the operation was indeed illegal; as one narrator notes: "When we arrived—it isn't important how, we didn't follow the most legitimate paths—and settled in, the first thing, of course, was to chop down the jujubes."[1]

The land these groups settled belonged to the Palestine Jewish Colonization Association (PICA), a society for settling Jews in the Land of Israel, founded in 1924. In 1900 Baron Edmond de Rothschild transferred management of the agricultural colonies he had founded in Palestine to the Jewish Colonization Association (ICA), which was founded in 1891 at the initiative of Baron Maurice de Hirsch. After the inauguration of the British mandate over Palestine, Rothschild resumed responsibility for the colonies and set up PICA as a subsidiary of ICA, with his son James as its president. ICA/PICA issued loans on affordable terms to settlers. Between 1936 and 1939, PICA was involved in the establishment of new settlements, including kibbutzim.[2]

At first the group worked the site on a temporary basis, with the consent of PICA. In 1940 the kibbutz "invaded" 1,125 *dunams* (about 280 acres) of PICA land, where its members uprooted a thick forest of jujubes that covered most of the plot. Their presence in Gennosar was legitimized and approved only after years of negotiations and squabbling with PICA and the rural settlement institutions.

In folklore studies, stories about the founding or initial settlement of a place are referred to as "legends of origin" or "legends of beginnings" (Bar-Itzhak 2001, 11–25). This genre, with its historical pretensions, is associated with a primal event in the narrator's geographical space, endowing it with a mythic quality. Modern Israeli scholarship and general intellectual discourse advocates appropriating the various Zionistic ideologies that motivated the Jewish population in Palestine in the prestate period, as well as the narratives associated with them and with the establishment of the Jewish state as "myth." In his book *The 1948 Generation: Myth, Profile, and Memory,* historian Emmanuel Sivan states: "To the Zionist myth of origin regarding the historical link to the land and the nation building enterprise was added a narrative about the establishment of the state in blood and fire" (1991, 13). Folklore scholars of the Zionist narrative use the term "myth" as well. For example, when Yael Zerubavel writes about the story of Tel Hai, she explicitly states that "every nation reconstructs its own past and creates its own 'myth of beginnings,' a sacred text about an early event in its history that presents a new paradigm in the life of the nation" (1991, 193).

The genre rests on an infrastructure of realia and endeavors to give a sense of credibility to the tale. The test of its success and its staying power derives from the fact that the stories are known and shared by people who live in the same region and share a common destiny or nationality. That group preserves the stories and passes them on. The oral traditions are reinforced by written sources that deal with local chronicles and by literature in general (Dorson 1972, 159–62). The concept of "legends of beginning" or "founding myths" leads to problems of which all folklore scholars are aware. These terms came into vogue when folklore studies were in their infancy and were applied to all stories with similar lineaments. The existence of ethnic categories and of the distortion that scholars might wreak on the culture being studied by applying terms that suggest fictiveness and variance with "the truth" to stories that the narrating society deems to be an integral part of its existential truth were ignored, however (Ben-Amos 1976, 215–42). In fact, every society treats its legends of origin as part of its authentic life. Any attempt to deny their veracity spawns fierce emotional opposition, fed by the feeling that the existential truth and world of sacred values are imperiled. As Lenn Goodman suggests, a "recognition of myth as a myth, that is a fiction, can diminish its power. When maximally effective, myths remain almost unnoticed" (1993, 107). The use made here of the terms "legends of beginnings" or "myth" is not meant to reject the authenticity of the stories, but precisely to emphasize the importance and sanctity ascribed to them by the narrating society.[3]

Members of the Kibbutz Gennosar identify the story of its settlement with what they call the "Sidriyot story" (the "jujube story"). Or as one narrator of the founding generation said: "All of us identify settlement and our first arrival on this plot of land with the Sidriyot [jujubes]. I don't know if there is another plant that has become a symbol like the jujube. One cannot think about Gennosar and settlement without the jujubes."[4]

The jujube, also know as the *Zizyphus spina-christi*, is a drupaceous tree or shrub of the family Rhamnaceae. It is thorny, with thick and tangled roots and fleshy, edible fruits. The jujube is native to Africa but became acclimated to Israel and is mentioned in the Mishna.[5] The Gennosar Valley had a dense covering of jujubes until about fifty years ago; the Arabs called them *sedar* (the tree) or *rubadiya* (the shrub). The jujube is a hardy tree and may live for a thousand years.

The tree is also a key symbol in the folk culture of Kibbutz Gennosar. A photograph of a jujube hung in the kibbutz dining hall for many years and is still included in various kibbutz publications. The "jujube song," written by a member of the kibbutz, used to be the quasi-anthem of Gennosar, and even today it is sung at the annual kibbutz festival. In the main, however, stories about the jujubes became the myth of the first settlement and founding of the kibbutz for all of its members, and for the second generation they provided nostalgic reminiscences of childhood. The stories told orally by members of Gennosar, as well as the versions written down in past years and preserved in the kibbutz archives and its various publications, indicate that the story has a polyphonic life.[6] Even though there are differences among the stories told by different narrators, and especially between those of the parent generation and their children, all of them are linked as a "dialogic narration" as this term is defined by Edward Bruner and Phyllis Gorfain (1984), who adopted the ideas of Mikhail Bakhtin (1981) about language and applied them to narration. Bruner and Gorfain maintain that a story cannot be viewed in isolation, as a monologic static entity, but must be seen in a dialogic or interactive framework; that is, "all stories are told in voices, not just structuralist oppositions or syntagmatic function of action. A story is told in a dynamic chorus of styles which voice the social and ideological positions they represent. Stories are polyphonic—they voice the narrative action, the reported speech of characters, the tellers' commentary, evaluative remarks, interpretive statements, and audience acknowledgment" (1984, 57.) Dialogic narration is expressed especially in the stories of the second generation. In their stories we find two perspectives: the one of the founders, with which they usually identify, together with their own unique perspective, which is sometimes different from that of the founders and indirectly even challenging it. The aggregate of the stories collected at Gennosar create a narrative of the local culture, a narrative in which the ethos of Zionist-socialist settlement, in all its complexity, is expounded for this particular kibbutz.

The following tale illuminates the story of settlement. I have chosen to present this particular variant from *Yisrael Levy of Gennosar* by Avshalom Tsoref because it is the earliest extant broad version.[7]

Early September is the season of deep plowing. By then we had to have the soil bare. It had been three years since the area had been traversed by man or beast. Back when they used to "politically plow" the field, they would prune back the jujubes. The women from the Arab village, too, used to cut off the thick branches and use them for firewood. During the last three years, it has become a tangled forest, a jungle of jujube trees and brambles.

. . .

It was a festive day for the group and for Yisrael.[8] The day the tractor arrived to begin the deep plowing in the jujube field, so did the five Gennosar prisoners.[9] The tractor arrived from Ashdot Ya'akov, fifty horsepower, gigantic by the standards of those days. With its deep plow it stood before the 500-dunam plot, ready to begin the assault on the ancient wasteland. Yisrael's plan was something like this: the tractor would move forward with a long harrow and pull out the jujube roots. It would be followed by the "infantry": four men to pile the roots on two wagons, hitched to two pair of mules. The jujubes would be stacked in the courtyard to be sold for firewood.

After the first short stretch it became clear that the idea failed to take account of the unknown variable hidden underground: the jujube roots were stronger than the steel of the plow, which shattered. The roots' capacity to hold on to the ground was greater than the 50 horsepower of the tractor. All our attempts were in vain.

For several days we tried to plow around the jujubes, to disengage the core of the root from those that branched and spread wide, to chain the root to the tractor and tug it out. We even tried explosives.

Then Yisrael tried the "irrigation method," in which you pour water all around the jujube. When the ground gets soft, you take a thick chain, which ends in a grapple that snags the root—and the tractor pulls. Sometimes the chain snaps, but sometimes the jujube is uprooted, taking a huge clod of earth with it and leaving behind a pit several meters in diameter. So we had a method, but the calculations were difficult and there was no water. What little we had was needed to water the other crops. This meant we had to haul in water, at first in barrels. But the pace was too slow and the tractor couldn't stand idle: every hour cost money.

We "drafted" the auto, managed to borrow a big tank, and began to dump water. The work was pursued with the stubbornness and diligence of ants. The tractor pulled with all its fifty horsepower and Yisrael helped with all his thousand manpower. Jujube after jujube was uprooted and the field got blacker and blacker.

The tractor was hooked up to the plow and began to till the bare soil. But it turned out there were still enough roots to break the plow. Zvi, the tractor driver from Ashdot, got caught up in the enthusiasm and stuck to the task. Seven times the plow broke and seven times was taken back to Ashdot to be welded.

There was already a significant plowed strip—real soil! The piles of jujubes were transported to the courtyard on sledges rigged up by Yisrael. The full manpower of the settlement was working in the field, with evening shifts and weekend shifts, while the auto was permanently assigned to the water detail, and the work moved forward, by the life of Heaven! . . .

At the beginning of December, the entire plot of 550 dunams had turned from a thicket of jujubes to a black plain. That month the group celebrated Hanukkah with a torchlight procession to dedicate the field. The torchlight procession continued well into the dark of night. During those days of battles on the Russian front, this demonstration was a sort of tangible symbol of lights piercing through and rising out of the darkness. . . . There was a feeling that, along with the uprooting of the jujubes, we had totally uprooted the question mark that had hovered over Gennosar for five years.

Yisrael Levy uprooting a jujube (Courtesy of Gennosar Archive)

All the stories about the uprooting of the jujubes are structured as legends of the origins of Jewish settlement in the Land of Israel and expressions of the Zionist ethos. This is manifested first and foremost in an act that alters the rural landscape. In the Gennosar tales, this is the act of uprooting the jujubes and turning the "forest of thorns into a flourishing garden," as one narrator puts it. The Zionist enterprise did indeed cause dramatic changes in the landscape and created not only facts on the ground, but also landscape myths (Bar-Gal and Shammai 1983). Among the best known of these myths are "draining the swamps" and "making the desert bloom."[10] In these stories of Zionist settlement, the settlers are described as redeemers who have come to restore the ancient visage of the land—the visage of the "land flowing with milk and honey." We must remember that the harsh conditions provided the settlers with a rude awakening. The disparity between expectations and reality was resolved by describing the Land of Israel as soil that the Bible had depicted as being fruitful in the past, but had become a wasteland ("the ancient wasteland" in the story quoted above) as a result of the destruction of its Jewish community and the exile of the people from their land. The renascent Jewish community was building a new man (who goes at it "with all his thousand manpower"), who, assisted by modern technology, would redeem the land and restore it to its past glory. Shaul Katz deals at length with the positive image of Eretz Israel in the eyes of the first settlers, who considered its visible desolation to be a transient phenomenon, in the specific context of the agricultural settlement at Petah Tikva. He shows that the underlying conception at that time was that knowledge acquired in Europe was an important source for advancing agriculture in Palestine (Katz 1982, 49–72). In the jujube stories, too, we find recurrent emphasis on the importance of the tractor, the bearer of technological progress, in the war against the jujubes.

Another aspect of the Zionist ethos reflected in the stories of the uprooting of the jujubes is that the deed is appreciated only if it involves extraordinary physical and emotional effort, if it is associated with tillage, and represents a revolutionary modification of the previous situation. Zionist settlement stories all express this approach in one fashion or another. Whether it is the draining of the swamps, the greening of the desert, or the construction of tower and stockade settlements, in all of them there is a revolutionary change that is esteemed because of the physical labor and effort involved, which is associated with cultivating the soil (cf. Bar-Gal and Shammai 1983; Katriel 1993, 116.) A large part of the story told above is devoted to a description of the extraordinary effort and persistence required to uproot the jujubes. All the stories include a detailed and sometimes even technical description of the tractor, the watering, and the uprooting; or, as one version concludes: "We shattered very many plows there, but in the end we managed to overcome the jujubes."

The revolutionary change that follows the uprooting of the jujubes is also highlighted in the various stories: the land turns from an ancient wasteland and a thicket of jujubes into a black plain. The torchlight procession becomes a tangible symbol of the lights piercing the darkness, while battles are raging on the Russian front. Most importantly, "there was a feeling that, along with the uprooting of the jujubes, we had totally uprooted the question mark that had hovered over Gennosar for five years."

The narrators employ language that endows the first settlers' deeds with a sacral dimension. The effort and tillage are described in terms taken from religious language. This reflects the sanctity that Zionism attributed to the act of settlement and tilling the soil, otherwise known as the "religion of labor." This use of language to sanctify settlement is also typical of other settlement stories, as was noted by Katriel and Shenhar in connection with the tower and stockade stories (1990, 368).

The story that symbolizes agricultural settlement at Gennosar is, accordingly, the story of the jujubes, or, in the words of the narrator quoted above: "All of us identify settlement and our first arrival on this plot of land with the jujubes." To be more precise, however, we should say that the story of agricultural settlement in Gennosar is identified with the *uprooting* of the jujubes. The story of the founding of Gennosar, which expresses the ethos of rebirth, is first of all a story of uprooting, although uprooting in order to plant a different species.

The fact that the founding of an agricultural community is symbolized by the uprooting of trees, in a region where trees are rare and precious, is significant. We must examine it in the light of three aspects. The first is the Jewish attitude toward trees in general and fruit trees in particular. Trees are a key symbol in the Bible—beginning with the Tree of Life and the Tree of Knowledge (Genesis 2:9). The power to create life inheres in trees (Genesis 1:29). Man is compared to a tree, and so are the people of Israel—to a grapevine, to a fig tree, and so on. Sons are compared to saplings, one's wife to a fruitful vine (Psalms 128:3). The ban on cutting down fruit trees is rooted in Scripture: "When in your war against a city you have to besiege it a long time in order to capture it, you must not destroy its trees, wielding the ax against them. You may eat of them, but you must not cut them down. Are trees of the field human to withdraw before you into the besieged city? Only trees that you know do not yield food may be destroyed" (Deuteronomy 20:19–20).[11]

Rabbinic literature is full of concern about damaging fruit trees, because of the ban known as "Do not destroy [foodstuffs]," as well as anxiety about the peril that uprooting trees may pose for human beings themselves. The Gemara (tractate Baba Kama 91b) relates that Rabbi Hanina attributed the death of his son to the untimely destruction of a fig tree (see also Baba Batra 26a). Jewish folklore frequently associates the human soul with that of trees. In *Pirkei de-Rabbi Eliezer* (chapter 34) there is an allusion to a tree's quasi-human vitality, expressed when it is cut down, much like the human soul departing the body: "When a fruit tree is cut down, a voice cries out from one end of the world to the other, but the voice is not heard. . . . And when the soul leaves the body, a voice cries out from one end of the world to the other, but the voice is not heard."[12] The intimate link between a settlement story and the up-rooting of trees could not fail to be problematic against the background of Judaism's attitude toward trees.

The second aspect we should consider is that afforestation and tree planting in the Land of Israel were a key element of the Zionist ethos. This element found strong expression in the folklore of the period in songs, stories, and customs. One of its central manifestations was the conversion of the minor holiday of Tu Bishvat (the fifteenth of the Hebrew month of Shevat), which in the Diaspora had been celebrated chiefly by eating fruits from of the Land of Israel, into a tree-planting festival. Thus, for example, Yehoshua Manoah describes how the holiday was spent in those days in the Jordan Valley: "It has become a custom in recent years for teachers in the rural settlements in the Lower Galilee to assemble their pupils on the fifteenth of Shevat and bring them to Deg-anya to plant trees there. . . . Even before sunrise the children are on the move. They come by foot, on horseback, and in wagons, with troupes of musicians leading them" (1971, 478).

Even though the interpretation that the narrating society gave to the story of the uprooting of the jujube trees was related to this ethos, in that the uprooting was understood to be preparing the ground for new planting of another sort, the very fact that the uprooting of the jujubes becomes a symbol of rebirth can only be viewed ironically against the background of this ethos.

The third aspect is the role of the jujube before the arrival of the Jewish settlers—in other words, its association with the Arabs. The lands that were taken over by the Gennosar settlers belonged to PICA and had previously been worked by Arab tenant farmers. The Arabs plowed between the jujubes. They lived in peace with the trees, which served them for many ends: their roots and pruned branches were used for firewood; their foliage provided shade in the summer; their fruit provided food; and their leaves and branches were used for medicinal purposes. Jamil Marii, who in this ethnography expresses the voice of the "other," told of his attitude toward the jujubes:

Sometimes my father says to me, "over there where the [kibbutz] vineyard stands, the jujubes were full, a veritable jungle of jujubes.

And then they [the Jews] uprooted them." They would uproot four or five jujubes a day. Go where there is an Arab village. You'll find jujubes there. Why? Because they provide shade all summer. We don't remove a jujube if it doesn't disturb us. We leave it there, fixed. We don't cut it down. If it gets in the way of work, or the house, then we uproot it. Only if there is no alternative. The jujube is very strong. It will grow back again from its root. (IFA 22834)

The Arab is characterized by his integration with the landscape. He lives in a sort of symbiosis with the jujubes.[13] The Jew, the new settler, is described as someone who wages war on the jujubes and overcomes them by means of metal implements, persistence, and ingenuity. The stories add the dimension of the titanic war between nature and culture.

The story of the uprooting of the jujubes is linked with the story of Jewish settlement, which also caused an uprooting—that of the previous residents—as well as the Jewish-Arab conflict in its local manifestations. The stories of the founders, the uprooters of the jujubes, are silent about this. Explicit statements of this aspect appear only in the stories told by the second generation. But even in the stories of the first generation, the plot and underlying stratum create a metaphoric analogy between Arabs and jujubes and build a quasi-mythical alliance between them. This alliance expresses the deepest feelings of the society, its almost primal fear of the other. The following two stories illustrate this point.

In those days, when we were living in Migdal, we had a high tower with a large spotlight on it that rotated and lit up the entire neighborhood, because the Arabs used to attack us all the time. Without warning there was an attack! I had to run to my position. I ran and ran. They had uprooted a jujube and I didn't know about it. I jumped right into it, into the thorns! The spotlight rotated and illuminated me. I tried to bend down so they wouldn't shoot at me, but I couldn't because of the thorns. I was stuck in the jujube! I thought I was a goner. When the attack was over I cried out to the gang and they managed to get me out.[14]

There's a story that I heard from Moshe Abas. It's about the period of the War of Independence, the period of the war. They [the Arabs] were bother-

ing us, we were bothering them. . . . That means there hardly was a night without shooting. Every night there was shooting, or they would shoot in the air and all sorts of things like that. One time they decided to attack the village in a way that would scare them [the Arabs] out of their wits. So there was one squad that was connected with Migdal. Fellows from Migdal and Gennosar. I think their leader was Yisrael Levy, Noa's father, the one who was killed, my uncle. And they attacked them. What the Arabs used to do is, around every house the sheep pen was surrounded by jujubes— not around the tent—but an enclosure of its own; they surrounded them with jujubes so the sheep wouldn't run away. They entered the village and started shooting and a firefight began. Exactly what happened there I don't know. Avigdor from Migdal, a fellow of twenty, was wounded, and they began to evacuate him. His wound was serious. He got entangled in a jujube with his clothes and belt in such a way that they absolutely could not free him, and they left him there. They [the Arabs] tortured him. He died. Today when I think about this, the jujube protected the Arabs. It caught that fellow and wouldn't let him go. It protected the Arabs.[15]

These stories follow ancient Jewish and Arab folklore motifs about people who are wounded after concealing themselves inside a tree. Both recount hostile actions. In the first story the Jews are attacked; in the second, they are the attackers. In both stories, the setting is defined by the jujubes. The first story takes place in the narrator's own space, which is characterized by an uprooted jujube. In the second story, set in the space of the other, the jujube is depicted as an integral part of the Arabs' lifescape, where it plays a known and defined role. Both stories present an armed confrontation between Jews and Arabs in which a Jewish protagonist is wounded. The Arabs and jujubes cooperate to wound him and are identified with one another. Both are threatening forces, although in the first story the protagonist manages to escape, whereas in the second the protagonist is wounded, tortured, and dies. The first story was recorded directly from Shulke Lupan, one of the founders of the kibbutz. The second story was recorded from Yovi Lupan, a second-generation narrator, as he heard it from one of the founders. In both the first and the second story, when relying on the founders' version the analogy is not stated directly. In the end of the second story, however, the second-generation narrator gives his own point of view—"When I think about this"—and makes a direct and explicit statement about the analogy between the Arabs and the jujubes.

As noted previously, jujube stories also circulate among the second generation at Gennosar, but with an added dimension. The story of the uprooting of the jujubes, an origins legend that this generation heard from their parents and retell in their own way, is accompanied by stories of a new sort about their childhood in the shadow of the jujubes. For the second generation, born at Gennosar, the jujubes are no longer a threatening reality that interferes with the birth of the new settlement. Those jujubes were uprooted by their parents; the few that remain are outside the settled portion of the kibbutz. Accordingly, walking out to the jujubes and playing in them was a pleasant adventure. When they tell these stories, the narrators are reliving their childhood and youth. Here are two examples of these second-generation jujube tales.

When we were children, there was a large stand of jujubes north of the din-ing hall, where the horsecane is today. There was a fence like this, and the horses would gallop there. In practice there were still jujubes in places they didn't need or where they didn't plow there so much. Dead areas of a sort. We used to make "houses." What does that mean? Every jujube has its own landscape and its own shape. We would clean up a little bit underneath it. We would spread a mat or a rug or something else and voilà! you've got a house. Our houses were in the jujubes. There were "secret jujubes." What's a "secret jujube"? Children of eight or ten have groups that fight against one [an]other. Each group had its own jujube and each jujube had its own secret. They would say: "Don't let on. That's our secret jujube."[16]

When I was born and a few years after that, when we started to go on outings by ourselves, by then there were no more jujubes in Gennosar. We had to take a walk to reach the jujubes. That was our regular hike every Saturday and of course we loved it. There were hardly any fruits in those years, and that was our fruit. So we walked out, picked the fruit, and ate it. We loved the fruit. When it falls from the tree and has time to dry, it was so sweet, sweet, sweet. I remember that there were no plastic bags then or anything to carry them in, so we would fill our pockets like this, or take our shirt, make a knot and fill it, and we would eat all week, until the next Saturday.

The most famous jujube, which was the largest, was the jujube in the bananas where the sheikh's tomb was. For years nobody touched it, probably because of the tomb. We would go there—and it was an entire world! First of all, it seemed as if we were very far from the settlement, because the road wasn't paved and hardly any cars traveled there—not like today, when it's a main artery; then it was very much isolated. In general, everything was wheat fields. You could lie down in the wheat and build houses and imagine you were in America, at least, in far-off and enchanted worlds. Hour after hour we would play in this place, and of course eat the sweet and tasty fruit. We thought it was so exotic and special then. We really thought so.[17]

As noted, the many stories of this type are imbued with the enchantment of the adult narrators' nostalgia for their childhood and youth. The stories show that the second, kibbutz-born generation accepts nature and the landscape symbolized by the jujube. For them, the jujube is a means of identification with the environment and asserting a sense of rootedness. This may be why they are more sensitive to the link between the previous natives and the place and why there is more empathy in their stories (as we shall see below). At the same time, the second generation gave greater expression to the problems and anxiety that the stories of the founder generation passed over in silence. This is demonstrated further by a comparison in the attitude toward the jujube fruit (the *Dom*) in their stories and in those of their parents. Eating the fruit occupies a central place in the second generation's stories, which frequently refer to its variegated flavors, but first-generation stories never mention eating the fruit. To tell the truth, the founders' stories never hint that the jujube is a fruit tree, whose drupes (the *Dom*) are sweet and nourishing and can be eaten if necessary. This can be explained only against the background of two aspects mentioned above, namely, the sense of guilt spawned by uprooting fruit trees, in contravention of Jewish tradition, and the clear association between the jujubes and the Arabs. The phenomenon may be similar to that noted by Tamar Katriel with regard to remarks by a member of Kibbutz Yifat, who, pointing to the olive grove next to the kibbutz museum, said: "I will never eat those olives. They're taboo for me. Those are olives *they* planted. How can I eat them?" (1993, 138).

As mentioned above, however, the second generation also tells the settlement story in a way that highlights the problem implicit in the founders' versions. In the second generation's stories, this problem, with its ethical and ideological overtones, takes on a mystical dimension and reflects the profundity of the irrational anxiety and sense of guilt and the need to justify the settlement enterprise. The Jewish-Arab struggle for the land is cast as a primordial struggle between culture, which subdued nature, and nature itself, which will arise one day to help its ancient allies and punish those who dared raise a hand against it. A number of stories make this point clear.

My mother always told us that when they lived in Migdal up on the hill and looked down at the valley, they saw it strewn with jujubes. There was almost nothing except for thorns and jujubes. In fact, when they came down to work here, the first thing they had to do was get rid of the jujubes, remove them. For us children, the jujubes were always some example of a rooted tree. In practice, if you know what a jujube is, it's roots that go very deep and branch out. It was not easy to remove them. Of course my father [Yisrael Levy] played a major role in the uprooting of the jujubes. There was no alternative; they needed open land to build and to till. That was impossible up on the hill, where there was an Arab village, Ro'er Abu-Shusha, so they had to build here in the valley.

For them [the founders' generation], the jujube symbolized the ability to overcome the difficulties of that time. Later it became some sort of myth in Gennosar; but that's what I understood, that was the message I got from the comrades. When they sang about how they had won out, because the jujube had very deep roots, when they uprooted the jujube, it was as if to say: "I am here!" The entire history of Gennosar is connected with the argument over the lands. Of course they took that [the Arabs] into account. But in those days they thought they were implementing Zionism. In my opinion, had the Arabs not acted aggressively toward Gennosar then, they would have reached agreements with them that would have been all to the

Arabs' good. They were very open, you see, according to the stories there was Yigal Allon, there was Ovadia S'hayek, who had friendly relations with them. But if they hadn't been aggressive, there wouldn't have been so many wars. But that was the period all over [the] country.[18]

At the beginning of the story the narrator's choice of words reflects the second generation's identification with their parents' deeds, which they view as an act of rebirth. The opening echoes Ezekiel's vision of the dry bones, which concludes with rebirth: "The hand of the Lord came upon me. He took me out by the spirit of the Lord and set me down in the valley. It was full of bones" (Ezekiel 37:1). But the rebirth, as envisioned by secular Zionism, is not the act of the deity, but the work of human beings—human beings who overcome the difficulties and proclaim: "I am here."

Nevertheless, it is impossible not to hear in the story a tone of self-justification: "There was no alternative." "Had the Arabs not acted aggressively toward Gennosar then, they would have reached agreements with them that would have been all to the Arabs' good." "But that was the period all over [the] country." The entire theme of subduing the land in the prestate period is extremely sensitive. With the perspective of time it arouses conflicting emotions—pride at the acts of the founders, whose deeds established "I am here," accompanied by feelings of guilt.

The Snake and the Jujube of the Tombs

In the plot alongside the Arab village (Plot 10), they left two or three very large jujubes standing together. Back then I never wondered why; it was a fact—they were still there. One day they dug a long ditch and laid some kind of pipe, and the ditch passed right through the jujubes. I was fifteen, already an amateur archaeologist. Wherever they dug, I was interested. During one of the rest breaks I went to see what was going on and walked through the entire length of the ditch. When I reached the jujube I realized that it stood atop graves, and this is why they hadn't chopped it down. On the surface they saw stones. A meter or so down was an Arab grave with bones. I examined it. I understood that it was an Arab grave, not all that old. I saw a skull. I cleaned the skull and saw that the eye was covered by a patch whose fabric had already rotted. There was a coin there, which I identified as a Turkish coin, and on top of it they had evidently sewn a black patch. I went further and again saw stones and a grave. For the first time in my life I said, I better look where I stick my hands. I looked and there was a snake there! (Not a viper, but a Montpellier snake).[19] *I looked at it and it looked at me, and then it retreated ever so slowly and vanished into some deeper place.* (IFA 22840)

The Doves' Jujube

We had a large jujube in the middle of the bananas. We called it the doves' jujube. This jujube was, overall, what shall I tell you, as big as from that chair over to here [indicating with his hands a distance of around twenty meters]. It covered a vast space. Lots of trunks came out of it. You would enter a sort of roof of jujube leaves, like a giant house, and the entire floor was full of drupes. We would walk out on Saturdays on purpose to gather drupes. We sewed ourselves nice bags and filled them with drupes. I knew the particular flavor of every jujube in the valley. Do you know that 99 percent of drupes have worms in them? I remember there were these "dainty" boys and girls who opened them up before taking a bite. I ate the drupes whole. When we grew up, in twelfth grade, something like that, and wanted to make a little money—even though they had taught us that that was forbidden—we invented a draft to cut down trees and sell them. We went to the doves' jujube and made a real mess there. One of the original comrades told me that the jujube had remained there for a good reason. There were tombs of Arab sheikhs around it. Really large tombs, piles of stone, so the Arabs never touched it. In my opinion, it was a sacred jujube. That same comrade told me that the jujubes symbolized the Arabs. You uproot it and it grows back. He believes that one day the Arabs will return to the jujube plots. I was away from Gennosar for 14 years. When I returned, in 1975, the jujube was gone. I looked into why they had uprooted the jujube, and the reason was—so that the Arabs wouldn't ask for the land. The doves' jujube is a symbol of my childhood, nostalgia for childhood. It was my bond with the place. For me a jujube is a special aroma, the pricking of the thorns, a special taste. (IFA 22841)[20]

Both of these stories radiate the anxiety that the Arabs might return to the place where the jujubes grew and claim the place as their own. In the first story this is expressed indirectly, whereas in the second it is stated explicitly.

In both of the above stories, fear puts on a largely supernatural guise. The story with the snake incorporates the motif, typical of both Jewish and Arab culture, of punishment for the profanation of a grave. True, the punishment does not actually take place, as in stories of that tale type; but the very fact that this story is told by a Jewish narrator who does not belong to a religious society can be explained only if the profanation of the grave is immoral in his own lights as well. Because it was his own society that perpetrated this deed, he finds himself in the conflict that produces the story.

In "The Snake and the Jujube of the Tombs," the uprooting of the jujube results in the discovery of an Arab grave. The snake, with the full load of symbols associated with it in Jewish culture, may connect the act with the primordial sin. The narrator is saved, because, for the first time in his life, he decides to look where he is sticking his hands. In other words, awareness of the danger that lurks deep underground around the jujube roots, the presence of the Arabs' bones, and the snake that has been delegated to guard the place are all parts of an ineluctable necessity. We have here a return of sorts to what we heard in the first generation's story of the uprooting of the jujubes: "The idea failed to take account of the unknown variable hidden underground." Even though the founding generation successfully uprooted the trees, in the story told by a member of the second generation, the unknown is still lurking in the depths of the earth. The snake does retreat deeper after the staring contest, but it remains there in the depths, its existence arousing emotions of both guilt and anxiety.

We should also note dialogic narration expressing the latent conflict between the first and second generations with regard to the uprooting of the doves' jujube at the end of the second story. The narrator asks why the jujube was uprooted and receives the explanation that it's to keep the Arabs from claiming the land. There is no actual conflict between the two generations, but the narrator's final words express grief and perhaps even a lament for this uprooting: "The doves' jujube is a symbol of my childhood, nostalgia for childhood. It was my bond with the place. For me a jujube is a special aroma, the pricking of the thorns, a special taste."

These stories inevitably arouse the question of how the tale is told on the other side, that is, in Palestinian society. The Palestinians abandoned the site during the War of 1948 and moved to Syria and Lebanon, so unfortunately I am unable to hear the story from them. We were able, however, to record the story as told by a member of a family who returned to the place.[21] The narrator, Jamil Marii, who was referred to above, has worked at Gennosar for many years. Of himself and his family he says: "We lived there in the Arab village of Majdal, my grandfather was fifth generation, here for generations, since the time of the Turks. The first ones [of Gennosar], Ovadia S'hayek and all that crew, lived in Migdal first before moving to Gennosar. Some of the land was PICA's, some belonged to the Arabs. My father worked at Gennosar starting in 1934, with the old-timers, like Ovadia S'hayek and Yigal Allon and all of them. He went with them to the end!"

This is Jamil Marii's story about the sheikhs' jujube:

There were sheikhs' tombs in the banana grove; it was called the cemetery. Every jujube was a hundred or two hundred years old, with huge branches, they almost covered five dunams. The last jujubes that were uprooted, it wasn't so long ago, in 1970. The kibbutz committee gave the order to get rid of the jujubes. Now, if you go to the jujubes where there used to be a grave, the bananas don't grow there. You can water the spot, but there's no grass. The ground, I don't know, the bunches are tiny. I work in the bananas. I go there. There's almost no grass. Those graves are ancient, perhaps from the time of Muhammad. The place isn't really good. (IFA 22842)

Here we have a sacred legend about punishment for the desecration of a holy tomb. Jamil sees here a conspicuous example of punishment for sin: the ground reacts to the uprooting of the trees by preventing growth. This is compatible with the idea, found in Palestinian folklore, that the jujube is a sacred tree and that a man who cuts it down can expect ill fortune (see note 13). Particularly prominent in Jamil's stories is the encounter between cultures. When he speaks about the uprooting of the jujubes, he says: "I don't think that the areas where the jujubes were will go back [to the Arabs]. That's finished. We're with the Jews until

the end. My father says, I hope you can die under the rule of the Jews."
But Jamil adds at once: "Land, the Arabs say, it doesn't matter who the
government is: Arab, Israeli, Turk, if they don't touch the women and
the land, let the authorities do what they want. They can be in control.
The land is my blood. It comes from my grandfather. Land cannot be
liberated."

On the one hand, Jamil accepts the hegemony of the kibbutz society with which he grew up. He and his family accepted the situation as
a matter of acquiescing in and relying on destiny. On the other hand,
Jamil is unequivocal and uncompromising about one thing—the bond
between the Arab and his land: "The land is my blood." This stance explains the anxieties we found in the kibbutz stories. The kibbutznik's
story of the sheikhs' (the doves') jujube is a reaction to the process of
internalizing the "other's" position and of the feelings that ensue.

To return to the kibbutzniks' stories and the jujube as a symbol,
it is a symbol of absence, of what no longer is. There are no jujubes at
Kibbutz Gennosar today. Against this background, there are interesting
stories about the second generation's attempt to restore the trees.

*When I was a preschool teacher, my sister Nitza and I tried to bring a ju-
jube and plant it outside the kindergarten. I planted all the seven species
and trees of the Land of Israel and decided that a jujube had to be there
too. However much we tried, though, we couldn't get it to grow. Nitza came
with a tractor and we dug. It's interesting: it was a tree with such roots that
it just had to succeed. Today there aren't any jujubes anywhere in Gennosar. There is one next to the archives. There are some in the neighborhood.
But in the kibbutz itself, none. This mission of preserving didn't work out
for me, for the two of us, actually. It symbolized the past and continuity. It's
a tree that as it were links what was and what will continue to be, links us
to the founders and to the future generations. The trees remain for generations. I really imagined that my children would pick the fruit and eat the
drupes. But it didn't work. We tried several times and it didn't work.*[22]

The attempt by the storyteller, Noa Kaplan, and her sister to plant a
jujube in Gennosar can be interpreted in a number of ways. The same
storyteller whose account of the uprooting of the jujubes insists that

through this act the founders were stating "I am here" now seeks to do just the opposite: to plant a jujube alongside the kindergarten. The context is important:[23] Noa decides there has to be a jujube there along with the seven species, that is, the fruits and grains for which the Land of Israel is renowned: "A land of wheat and barley, of vines, figs, and pomegranates, a land of olive trees and [date] honey" (Deuteronomy 8:8). From this perspective, her act is the antithesis of the founders'; that is, she is recognizing the natural place of the jujube in the landscape of the country and is even endowing it with additional holiness by associating it with the seven species. But there is another context here as well: Noa's desire to restore the jujube to the kibbutz is motivated by her aspiration to create a bond between the deeds of the founders, the fathers, and the younger generation. The narrator, who is an educator, understands the importance of what Bruner and Gorfain call the experiential dialogue between the self and society (Bruner and Gorfain 1984, 72–73). The absence of the jujube as symbolizer diminishes the meaning of the symbol. The children simply can no longer see, touch, feel, or taste the fruit of the jujube. Clearly the absence of any chance of experiential dialogue imperils the dialogue with the deeds of the founders, which is threatened with being consigned to oblivion by the younger generation.

The very willingness to restore the jujube indicates not only acceptance of the natural landscape of the country, but also a feeling of security: there is no more danger lurking in their shade. The anxiety that the Arabs may come back and claim the land on which the jujubes are growing is fading away. If the jujube that would grow in Gennosar could be the one planted by the members of the kibbutz, it would solve some of the second generation's problems regarding the jujube as symbol. It would legitimize their identification with the jujubes and make their wish and claim, that the jujubes are "ours," a valid one. At the end of a story told by one narrator of the second generation she says provocatively, attributing the jujube to her generation:[24] "The jujube is ours. I don't know who fought for it, who planted it. It's part of us. I can dispute with any Arab today that it's mine as much as his. My childhood and my roots are associated with that jujube. The second generation that grew up here, it speaks to them a lot."[25] We have to be very careful discussing the second generation's identification with the previous natives. True, their identification with the landscape of the country and the jujube leads to understanding of the former natives' attachment to the land. But they view this landscape as part of their own life. On the other hand, the fact that the jujube does not grow, even though one would have expected it to strike root because of the nature of the plant, is interpreted in the story as a punishment. This clearly reflects a sense of guilt about the fathers' deed, alongside all the shades of meaning associated with the jujube as a key symbol in the folk culture of Kibbutz Gennosar.

Sherry Ortner, in her discussion of key symbols, demonstrates that some symbols seem to summarize what the entire system represents. These are sacred symbols that are woven into the complex system of ideas in a way that unifies the entire system (1973).[26] The narrative built by the jujube stories of Kibbutz Gennosar point to the complexity of the jujube as a symbol: the conquest of the soil and building of the settlement, heroism and self-sacrifice, uprooting and planting, nature and culture, Jews and Arabs, childhood and adventure, pride, anxiety, and guilt and more. The jujube becomes a key symbol as the communicative connection between worlds that have different contents, a symbol that by its nature contains a whole slew of simultaneous meanings and ambiguities. As a folklorist it was important for me to construct this ethnography by presenting the stories of various narrators and listening closely to the unique voice of each one. Nevertheless, focusing on each story in isolation from the others would have missed the objective I set for myself in this ethnography. The adoption of Mikhail Bakhtin's concept of "dialogic narration," as applied to the study of cultural narratives by Bruner and Gorfain, made it possible to study the dialogue carried on among the various stories, especially between those related by the founding generation and the successor generation. This permitted the construction of the narrative of the local culture as a polyphonic narrative, in which the jujube serves as a complex key symbol. Unlike the great national narratives of Israel, such as the "draining of the swamps" and "tower and stockade," the Gennosar stories hardly ventured beyond the confines of the community in which they were created and told. Nevertheless, their study shows that the local narrative, ostensibly marginal, encompasses and expresses the full complexity of the ideological narrative of Zionist-socialist rural settlement in the Land of Israel, from which it grew and which in turn it nurtured. In this way the jujube stories of Gennosar exemplify the importance of local legends for cultural interpretation.

2
Processes of Change in the Kibbutz as Reflected in Local Legends

A variety of legends about people and events are associated with Kibbutz Ein Harod. With regard to their genre, it is convenient to call these stories "historical legends." Although some of the stories being told in that community today were circulated there in the past, others were never told in the past, even though they deal with personalities and events from that time. Moreover, the people and events featured in these stories were formerly viewed as better passed over in silence; the community could not accept such people and events, and weaving stories about them was considered to be illegitimate. Such stories are a new phenomenon that expresses the contemporary situation, when the society feels a need to produce stories about people and events from its past as a way to express the changes it is experiencing in the present. Nevertheless, creating stories set in the recent past is not the only way a society may express its problems, adversities, yearnings, and hopes. It is often easier and more convenient to express such concepts through a narrative plot implanted in the distant past.

As mentioned below, today the kibbutz often finds itself at a crossroads as a result of changes in the Israeli society, as well as far-reaching changes and conflicting orientations within the kibbutz society. The question arises if and how folklore, as the cultural infrastructure of society, reflects these changes and provides the means to express them. To answer this question, it is helpful to look at the findings from a study of narratives told by a kibbutz storyteller. The narratives were analyzed by examining their symbolism and their archetypical infrastructure, as well as by examining the viewpoint from which the narrative was being presented.

The first days of Ein Harod (Courtesy of Ein Harod Archive)

Ein Harod is one of the older kibbutzim. It was established in 1921 by members of the Gedud Ha'avodah, the Labor Brigade (Yanai 1971).[1] The degree of symbolism attributed by Israeli society to this kibbutz is perhaps evidenced by the fact that an Israeli author, Amos Kenan, chose to name his book, which constitutes a kind of apocalyptic vision of the future of Israel, *The Road to Ein Harod.* The kibbutz produced a number of prominent personages, some of whom became national symbols in Israeli society, such as Haim Shturman, Yitshak Tabenkin, Shlomo Lavie, and Aharon Zisling. The history of the kibbutz is marked by tragic changes—as a split on ideological grounds that occurred in the 1950s led to the breaking up of families, to the establishment of two separate kibbutzim, and to bitterness and hostility that has not subsided up to this very day. Another tragic dimension is added by the large number of native kibbutz members who fell in the Israeli wars.[2] As one of my interviewees said to me as we were walking along the paths of the kibbutz: "Do you feel the sadness? These are our longings for the sons who fell, they hover in the air and create the atmosphere of Ein Harod."[3]

Yair Benari, the narrator on whose stories I base the following discussion, belongs to what is called the first generation of children who were born in the kibbutz, and he was in his mid-sixties when he told

A festival in Ein Harod, 1925 (Courtesy of Ein Harod Archive)

Ein Harod, 2000 (Courtesy of Ein Harod Archive)

the stories. Before the War of Independence started, he joined the Palmach,[4] served in the Israel Defense Forces as a company commander, and fought in several wars. He served as a guide, youth counselor, and teacher and held several appointments in the kibbutz and the kibbutz movement. He is known as a storyteller, and in addition to spontaneous events, he is usually invited to narrate on formal occasions, such as the anniversary of the kibbutz, bar mitzvah ceremonies, and other events. Benari himself identifies with the role of a storyteller: "At one time, people in the kibbutz said I ought to write down things. 'You remember so much, why not write it down?!' they would say. Okay. Actually, I did write down things, trying to shape them and make them literary. It's all been recorded in writing; you can come and see for yourself. But there is no melody to it."

Two types of tales can be distinguished in Benari's narrative repertoire. Some of his stories were recounted in the kibbutz almost from its earliest days, continue to circulate orally, and have even been transcribed and published in various forums. He recounts them on various occasions, always, of course, in his own unique fashion. Other stories are those that were not told in the past; with them, the storyteller sees himself as rescuing the people and events involved from the gulf of oblivion. The two types of stories have different functions to perform.

The first type of stories express the tendency to mythicize the kibbutz.[5] These stories build the kibbutz mythologically, in the sense that the original factual nucleus (which is always there) is elaborated on, expanded, and interpreted, and in the process of doing so an epic meaning is given to it. The narration of the events and the interpretation accompanying it add dimensions larger than is warranted by the real event. The heroes rise beyond the level of ordinary human characters and become larger than life. Here is an example of such a story.[6]

The Story of Shlomo Lavie and His Sons

I remember Lavie well. It is impossible to forget him. I think that the idea of Ein Harod and the deed of Ein Harod have several progenitors. Over time, it is today fairly correct to view Lavie as the father of the idea of Ein Harod. It is quite possible that many people will say he was not the only one, that there were many. One person contributed something, and another person contributed something else, and Lavie contributed something in addition to all this . . . Maybe. Perhaps Ein Harod is a creation that was not fathered by just one person. Ein Harod is not a child. But you have to be aware of the important place occupied by Lavie. I can tell you thousands of stories about his two sons. Yerubaal was the kind of person who loved peace and pursued peace. Hillel was fighter. Yerubaal was the first to fall. He fell in the battle for Mount Gilboa. After Yerubaal fell in this battle, thirty days after he died, the Kibbutz administration put up a notice on the notice-board. The notice read: "Memorial services will be held for our son Yerubaal; May God avenge his death," the familiar Jewish saying. The notice-board was inside a small shack, if you remember, at the north entrance, that is where they put up the notice. We used the north entrance to get to the dining hall—that is where they put up the notice. Hillel took a pencil, struck out the words "May God avenge his death," and wrote instead, "We shall avenge his death."

We, the people of Ein Harod—we need not tell the story of Yerubaal's death in the battle of Mount Gilboa early in the Month of Adar, 1948. It happened on a Friday. The body was placed on a bench from the dining hall that had been taken to Lavie's room, the body was with all his clothes on, it was covered with an army blanket, until they would bury him. There are people among us who have lived through this. And suddenly the son, Hillel, rises, who had been sitting beside the father, beside the body of his brother, and he said to the father: "I am going." (This means "I am going to fight in the war.") He sounded so determined, as though he was saying, "Do not try to stop me, do not try to hinder me." Lavie stood up (I was there at that very moment), and the two of them stood there, father and son, next to the body of Yerubaal, and they were holding hands, the two of them were each holding the two hands of the other, and Lavie said to Hillel: "Go, my son, go." That's it. Four words. And Hillel went to the war. He did. Hillel did. And a few months later Hillel fell in the battle of Kfar Darom. We know it, we do. (IFA 22844)

Kirk points out (1970) that myth addresses the emotional level of the human condition and that it projects images that elicit either identification or rejection, admiration or alienation. Myth is dramatic work, and as such it needs heroes. Lavie and his two sons are the heroes of the Ein Harod myth. Myth deals with imagery, that is, with symbolic language, and it is grounded in the existential archetypes of the narrating society. In trying to uncover the system of images and archetypes in our story, we find at the base of the story the most archetypal and central nucleus of Jewish society—the story of the Akeda, "the binding," or the sacrifice of Isaac. In the biblical story, Abraham, the forefather, is told: "Take your son, your only son, whom you love, Isaac, and go to the land of Moriah and offer him there as a burnt offering upon one of the mountains of which I shall tell you" (Genesis 22:2). And Abraham carries out the command, making the journey to Moriah with his son so that he may sacrifice him to God.

However, the ancient tale of Abraham's sacrifice takes on a new shape in the kibbutz myth, turning into a secular Israeli story of the sons' sacrifice. In the story of Lavie and his sons, the biblical tale is expressed through the comprehensive structure of a father who sacrifices his sons, and through the use of imagery connoting the biblical Abraham. Also, both stories feature a mountain to delineate the spatial aspect—Mount Moriah in the Bible, and Mount Gilboa, at the foot of which Ein Harod is located, in the Lavie story.

Yet an analysis of the kibbutz tale uncovers the basic difference in worldview expressed in the two stories, which comes out against the background of an analogy. Abraham is commanded by God to sacrifice his son; the purpose of the command was to put his religious faith to the test. In Lavie's story, the decision rests with Man, and the cause for the action is the War of Independence, fought to defend the country in which a national home for the Jewish people is to be created. Even at the opening of the story, the symbolics of the New Jew, the Israeli, are present. Hillel erases the sentence "May God avenge his death" from the death notice, and writes "We shall avenge his death" instead. The act is of central importance. The original sentence customarily follows the name of persons who were killed or murdered, as the Jewish religion prohibits human vengeance. None but God may avenge a man's death. Hillel's bold rewriting of these significant words is symbolic of the approach taken by the Zionist movement. For two thousand years, religious Jews in the Diaspora wished to return to the Land of Israel, but they made the return conditional upon the myth of the coming of the Messiah, at a time decided upon by God. Conversely, the Zionist movement took the approach that the return to the Land of Israel is redemptive on the national level, as distinct from the religious level, and it is therefore to be achieved by Man.

Lavie is ready to sacrifice his sons, not for a religious concept, but for the value of nationalism, which the Zionist movement had made the center of its goal. Lavie's experience and his suffering are believed to surpass the trial that was imposed on Abraham. Abraham was told to sacrifice one son, but Lavie is ready to send also his second son to fight—the one and only son left to him. Again, Abraham was put to the test, but at the end God sent him a ram that he sacrificed instead of his son Isaac. Lavie's sacrifice is real, and as Israeli kibbutz society is decidedly secular, there is no prospect of a miracle to save the sons' lives.

Yet the main difference between the two stories is found in the sons' roles. The biblical Isaac is passive. He does not know where his father is taking him, and the fact that he is unaware of what is going to happen to him is dramatically reflected in the question: "The fire is there, and the pieces of wood are there, but where is the lamb for a burnt offering?" In contrast, Lavie's sons are active. Yerubaal is killed in the War of Independence, in the battle of Mount Gilboa, and Hillel will replace him. The two sons are ready to be the "burnt offering" sacrificed for the Jewish national home. In doing so, they act in perfect—and painful—harmony with their father's generation; this is the meaning of the scene in which Lavie and Hillel are holding each other by both their hands as they stand beside Yerubaal's body.

According to Sherry Ortner's definition, the "root metaphor formulates the unity of cultural orientation underlying many aspects of experience by virtue of the fact that those many aspects of experience can be linked to it" (1973, 1340). The story undoubtedly reflects the worldview of the narrating society—in this case, the central symbolics or the "root metaphors" (Pepper 1942; Ortner 1973) of secular-Zionist workers and settlers in the land of Israel.

The modern story of "the binding" as an existential archetype manifests itself in various forms in Israeli culture and is expressed in literature, in the visual arts, and in film.[7] Side by side with the story as a tragic and collective myth (Abraham Shlonski, Yitshak Lamdan), the story of the binding is also found as a private-personal myth (Natan Alterman, Haim Gouri, Tuvia Rivner), as an absurd command (S. Yizhar, Meir Wiseltier). We also find demythicization of the binding (A. B. Yehoshua, Amir Gilboa) and protest against the binding as an existential metaphor (Yehuda Amichai, Yitshak Laor). Many see time as the central variable that influences the character that the story of the binding assumes in

Israeli culture, from a collective myth in the past to a protest story in the present. It seems that time is only one variable, although its significance should not be denied. But even today the story's many manifestations are influenced by context in its broad sense, that is, by the narrator, the audience, and the situation. The story is multivoiced in Israeli culture, and all versions constitute an expression to the voice of Israeli culture.

The story of the binding of Ein Harod is told even today as both a personal and collective myth. I have not found any versions of demythicization or protest. Even if we say that protest exists, that it is expressed in the fact that young people do not customarily tell this story, and that it is told only in formal frameworks (school) and in formal narrative situations, such as memorial days and visits to cemeteries, it is clear that the children of Ein Harod grow up and are educated according to the values the story represents, and that members are constantly reexposed to the story on set dates during the course of a year. The story, to use the language of Mircea Eliade (1968, 15), is a ritual that enables the return and the renewal of times of inception. It connects the historical time to the beginning of the kibbutz, and thus it attempts to capture the constant value of the elapsing and endows meaning to the life of the individual and of the group.

In order to learn about additional symbols in the stories of mythicization let us consider the following story told by Yair Benari.

Walking Barefoot in the Land of Israel

I would like to tell you a story I have called "Walking Barefoot in the Land of Israel." These are not things invented by me. I did not write books or write eulogies or notes or a diary. I did not deviate from local standards. Perhaps this is the good part of me that I remained a local narrator. I would like to relate things that I did not invent, but rather, words spoken by Maletz, great words.

When Rafi Maletz, David Maletz's son, fell in battle, his father read a eulogy, which in my opinion is most interesting. The eulogy does not appear in the book memorializing him. The book was published about two or three years after his fall in battle, but the eulogy was not included in it. It lives only in my memory and in the memory of a few other people who were present at that time. . . . The event took place in the dining room, and there were many people present, and it was there that he spoke. The words he spoke should be preserved, and in this matter we are perhaps not different from past generations. What is really good is preserved. He said: "I grew up abroad, and here I was among the founders of Ein Harod, of the Third Aliyah. A child growing up abroad knew that in a Jewish town, he would receive his own bookshelf. A child in his own environment had his own bookshelf. And as he grew up, for every occasion his parents or uncles and aunts added something. Another book to his bookshelf. His private one. The child was able to imbibe from somewhere, from what was found on his bookshelf.

"And so we established a kibbutz here, a new phenomenon. And we enrolled the children in a communal educational setting and deprived them of having their own bookshelf. The child grew up without private property, but also without a private bookshelf. And I was always afraid," said Maletz in eulogizing his son, "I was always afraid that our children would grow up insensitive . . . I was worried. I am a booklover . . .

"But now, as I read my son Rafi's letters, I say: 'This boy grew up without his own bookshelf. This boy walked across the land of Israel barefooted and felt the earth with his bare feet.' Perhaps this barefooted walking across the Land of Israel was his bookshelf." (IFA 22845)

The structure of "binding" is found in this story too by the very fact that a father is eulogizing his son who fell in battle in the War of Independence. But this eulogy exposes another aspect in the symbolics of the kibbutz. Maletz, the father, a bibliophile and a writer in his own right, is expressing his inner debate in everything regarding the education of the kibbutz children. This struggle was expressed widely in the *Yishuv* before the War of Independence with regard to the character of the Sabra generation as a closed and insensitive people.[8]

In this story, the lack of private property, which is the foundation of socialist ideology of the kibbutz, is viewed as a disadvantage and as a contradiction to a sacred Jewish value—the bookshelf. Books are a concrete expression to spiritual values the individual acquires for himself while reading. The book, the supreme spiritual value in traditional Judaism, is replaced by the Land of Israel and the man connecting to it by his barefoot walking on its earth. This walking is an expression of a man who fills the earth anywhere, a man rooted in his earth, which the Zionist movement as a whole and the working settlers in particular sought to create. This trend was concretely expressed in the kibbutz. The children used to walk barefooted in the kibbutz and on frequent nature excursions all over the country. Expressions such as "to conquer the country with your feet"[9] or "to love the country through your feet" are common in the language of the narrator and are attributed to the teacher Moshe Carmi, who also acquired dimensions of a mythical figure in his stories.[10]

Rafi's death puts an end to his father's inner struggle and sanctifies the value he actualized.[11] The earth he was connected to during his life is the land he died for and in which he is buried. His walking barefoot in the Land of Israel becomes a symbol, and the land, the earth, is sanctified and rises to a level of supreme value. A new theodition is created, "Theodition having national and secular character" (Sivan, 1991, 174–82). The words *nation, homeland, the Nation of Israel,* and *the Land of Israel* have become key words in the new martyrology.

Rafi, Hillel, and Yerubaal, like their other friends who fell in battle, are the young heroes forever in the collective memory of Ein Harod—those who walk barefoot on its earth, fearless, assured of themselves and of their worldview. Unlike their living friends, they did not have to compromise and to adapt themselves to the changing reality and changing values of Israeli society. Thus they themselves became the symbol for the values of the founders, and their deaths sanctified these values.

In all the kibbutz stories, the values chiefly mythicized are heroism and sacrifice; the tales center on acts of bravery performed by the earliest settlers or by the next generation, these are the "key symbols" (Ortner 1973). The functions of these stories in kibbutz society are similar to the functions of myths in all societies. The stories have a sort of interpretative, evaluative function that involves understanding life and giving life meaning (Kolakowski 1989, 16). The stories interpret life in the kibbutz society, and they furnish the concepts that enable the kibbutz members to understand the present while elevating the past to the level of sacredness.

An operative function serves to underpin both individual and group behavior. The behavioral pattern represented by the myth is regarded as fit for imitation, and it legitimizes the values, the norms, and the social order; at the same time, a climate of opinion is created that enables the people living in the kibbutz to accept their way of life and be ready to defend those values.

Side by side with mythicization, the narrative repertoire of the storyteller also tends to do the reverse: there are stories that aim at demythicization. There are other kibbutz storytellers who equally tend to demythicize, but this storyteller, Yair Benari, seems to do so thanks to his special personality.

When I was eight or nine years old, Haim Shturman the grandfather was killed, and they placed his body in the reading room of Ein Harod. On this day, all the members of the kibbutz sorrowed; it was a great day, a day of a kind festive mourning. It is hard to explain, but Haim Shturman was not an ordinary average person.

The members were milling around, and I—a boy of eight—was there too, and my imagination was working overtime. Haim Shturman had been a smoker, he had been a cigarette addict. When I remembered Haim Shturman, I remembered him with a cigarette in his mouth. I always remembered how he used to throw a cigarette butt on the ground and stamp it out with his heel. As his body was lying in the reading room, I walked about and—the imagination of an eight-year-old—I thought maybe the cigarette was not extinguished, maybe there was a spark, and if I would find his cigarette, something that was still alive, I would breathe life into it, and Haim Shturman would live. I did not find a cigarette butt.

And then the family arrived. Atara came in. She was the woman about whom Yoram Kaniuk wrote that she was the uncrowned queen of her generation. And Atara stands up and says: "In this family we don't cry."

I want to switch to a related matter. In our family, my father left my mother and went to live with another woman, and they raised a family. His funeral started in Ein Harod Yihud. They placed the coffin in the dining hall and the members filed by, and then they carried the coffin to Ein Harod Me'uhad.[12] The funeral was impressive. My mother did not come to the funeral. She did not come. And I noticed that she was conspicuous for her absence. As soon as I came back home after the funeral, I went up to her room and I said: "I understand that you could not go, that it was hard for you, but did you see the funeral?" She replied: "Of course I did. I was sitting at the window all the time and watching. They moved from our part of Ein Harod to your part. I kept looking all the time. And I am not that kind of person. If he had lived with me, I would have screamed." And I live, so to speak, between Atara Shturman, who said that "in our family we don't cry," and my mother, a simple woman, who said "if he had lived with me, I would have screamed." (IFA 22846)

This revealing story, which reflects the world of the storyteller, combines two things: mythicizing and demythicizing. On the one hand, there is the mythic image of Atara Shturman (who deserves special mention in her own right). She stands for the values of heroism and self-control, which the kibbutz movement prized highly over a period of many years. When someone was buried, there was complete silence, and the honorable way of parting from a loved one was to exercise self-restraint. The one feature that is given prominence is the will to build the New Jew, who is the antithesis of the Diaspora Jew, who weeps and wails.[13] The story about the narrator's mother shows that the kibbutz was never made up from one kind of people only. Not all the members were Atara Shturman, and not all the members believed people must conduct themselves the way she did. The story reflects a large measure of mythoclasm—it erodes the myth of ideological and social homogeneity.

The story also exposes the inner world of the narrator, the sensitivity of the storyteller as a child, and his self-image regarding his place in the kibbutz society. He is a man standing between two worlds. On the one hand, he admires the values embodied in the image of Atara Shturman by which he was raised in the educational framework of the kibbutz, but on the other hand, he identifies with and is able to appreciate the position of his mother, "a simple woman," in his words. This ambivalence is without doubt one of the factors for the stories of mythicization and demythicization found side by side in the narrator's repertoire.

Nevertheless, most of the stories of demythicization belong to the second type in the storyteller's narrative repertoire. As noted above, these are stories that simply were not told in the past, even though they deal with personalities and events from that past. Today Yair Benari recounts them chiefly during the guided tours of the old cemetery of Ein Harod that he conducts for groups and individuals. The cemetery, which contains 140 graves (not all of them of members of the kibbutz), served Ein Harod for sixteen years, between 1922 and 1938.

The old cemetery of Ein Harod (Courtesy of Ein Harod Archive)

Benari's testimony does not make clear when he first became interested in these graves. The book by his father, Nahum Benari, published in 1931, includes short biographies of several of the people who are buried in the old cemetery. Perhaps his interest was aroused when he first read the book, many years ago. There is no doubt, however, that his vivid interest in this cemetery, which ultimately spawned the guided tours and the stories told during them, began in 1984, when he helped his daughter, a high school senior, write a term paper about the old cemetery. The storyteller took the project seriously; the intensive encounter between the father and his daughter and her friends, members of the younger generation of Ein Harod, influenced the centrality of these stories in his narrative repertoire and the unique perspective from which he chose to recount them.

One of the kibbutz myths is the ever-present spirit of nobility of the early settlers. The myth was reinforced by the committed Hebrew literature of those days (Knaani 1986). The hardships, the backbreaking work in a climate the pioneers were not used to, and the attempt to create something ex nihilo—all of these were described as the manifestations

Yair telling a story in the old cemetery (Courtesy of Ein Harod Archive)

of a true nobility of spirit. The scenario involved pioneers who worked very hard and had very little to eat, yet would assemble in the evenings and dance the Hora till late at night—in an elated frame of mind.

With this background in mind, here are the stories used by the narrator, Yair Benari, in the old cemetery of Ein Harod to open and close his guided tours.

Nahman Gellerman

The first grave whose tombstone is documented and about which there is written material is that of Nahman Gellerman. The date is Tevet 5,682 (1922). Ein Harod was founded on the 18th (or 12th–19th) of Elul 5,681 (1921). That is to say, after four months, the man was buried. He was twenty-four when he died.

It was a painstaking task to try to discover traces of Nahman Gellerman.

In the play "The Twentieth Night" by Yehoshua Sobol (following the publication of the book on the beginnings of Ha'Shomer Ha'Tsair), there are descriptions of attempts of total exposure of people. "Gedud Ha'Avodah" began in a different manner.

One of my sources for information, as yours, was my home: my mother, my father, the people close to me. My mother told me on several occasions that regarding private matters of a fellow, it was inappropriate to enter a man's garden with boots or work-shoes on. This, in contrast to Sobol's play, in which everyone opened himself up to the maximum.

Once we used to sing:

> *Comrade Berl, an old-timer worker,*
> *Does no good but does no harm.*
> *This is the strength of the* kevutsah . . . *(group, commune)*

In the Gedud Ha'Avodah, there were more than 50 percent of the type of "Comrade Berl," who does no good but does no harm and is not chosen according to any criteria of the movement, and he merely joins the group.

Whether in this lay the strength of the group (kevutsah) is another matter for argument. But there were many such "Comrade Berls."

Thus, when you come and wonder, Nahman Gellerman, the man has died and no one knows whether he has any relatives. Does he have parents? Who should be notified of his death? Nothing at all! He was in the Gedud Ha'Avodah for one year; he came with the group and arrived at Ein Harod. And here, for reasons not understood by anyone, he became severely despondent and depressed. No one was interested, not because he was not an interesting person, but because people decreed on themselves that it was not allowed to enter another's soul "with boots on."

The only story I have found about him was that a few days before his death, he asked to be assigned to guard-duty. This, of course, does not teach us anything about him, but nevertheless, he asked to be assigned to guard-duty. The guard used to walk all night armed. At 5:30 in the morning, the bell would ring and wake up the members in the camp to work.

If I were to use the language of that period, I would say that Nahman Gellerman fulfilled his duty to the end. He still rang the bell at 5:30 to wake up everyone to work. Only after that, he took the gun he had used for guarding, aimed at his temple, and killed himself.

And no one could explain why. He did not share his distress with anyone. The members did not even know whom to notify. Certainly he did not come from the "Holy Spirit." He must have had parents. He had a family. He came from somewhere.

I am trying to tell about early beginnings, about living people, trying to paint them as living characters. But this event which took place weighs heavily on us and follows us. (IFA 22847)

Who is Nahman Gellerman? By the criteria of the founders, he is a figure who deserves to be belittled. In a heroic period, there is no room for an antihero. Nahman Gellerman is a man who failed, and the extremists would perhaps even say a man who betrayed an idea, a mission, and yielded to his personal frailties. When the narrator chooses to tell the story of Nahman Gellerman to groups or to individuals with whom he tours the old cemetery, he takes a stand whose meaning is: there is room for telling about those antiheroes. They too were part of the group (the *kevutsah*) and contributed toward its existence. The very act of story-telling is an answer to the question posed in it: what is the strength of the commune? Like other figures who were called in the quoted poem "Comrade Berl," Nahman was part of the strength of the group. The act of guarding, waking up members to their daily work, and the use of a pompous style of the founders' period "fulfilling their duty to the end," which was used for noting the heroism of those who fell in the line of duty, are also intended to constitute testimony to Gellerman's con-tribution. Beyond conjuring up the image of Nahman Gellerman, the story expresses a penetrating criticism of the founders, those who did not see, did not ask, did not know, and did not tell, because they decreed on themselves not to touch personal matters. By using a large number of short interrogative sentences, the narrator presents a large question mark regarding the behavior of the founders. There is a difference be-tween a decree a person subjects himself to in avoiding dealing with delicate matters and the hardness and opaqueness to which this decree leads. This hardness does not gain forgiveness in the story, and the nar-rator presents it as a blot hanging over the kibbutz, even in subsequent generations, and uses the plural in saying: "This event which took place weighs heavily on us and follows us."

The Graves of the Children

Now we are leaving the old cemetery of Ein Harod, and we are on the burial ground where the children were interred. Here there are just a few heaps of stones, unmarked, without any inscriptions. There is nothing like this anywhere else—perhaps there are one or two more burial grounds like that in Israel. In the old cemetery of Zikhron Ya'akov there are unmarked graves of children that have no tombstones. Perhaps in some other places— very few places. This is very unusual indeed. I would almost say this is an un-Jewish way of doing things. The question arises—why should this be so? I don't know if you know this, but there was one more child between my sister and myself. This child was buried here. He is one of these heaps of stones. If he had lived, he would be the same age as Yoseph Reichenstein. He even had a name. Sometimes, my mother made a mistake and called me by his name. Every year, at least once, I would go there with my mother. Even then, we could not find the spot where he was buried. Even when I was a child I wondered why there were no tombstones. I never got an answer to my question. My mother would say that in those days they used to say there will be another child, and the parents would be comforted—no need for a tombstone, there is going to be another child.

Some older members of Ein Harod try to explain away the pathetic little heaps of stones on the children's graves by pointing out that in those days they were living in extreme poverty. The conclusion to be drawn is this: As opposed to the romantic notion of ennobling poverty, in life poverty does not ennoble, but degrade. (IFA 22848)

In this story the narrator touches a deep pain, which constitutes "exposed nerves" at least for some of the kibbutz members. Benari integrates his own personal story, whose protagonists are his dead brother, his mother, and himself, into the general story, thereby giving it an extra measure of pathos and authenticity. The question posed by the story is this: was the heroic period one mainly of exaltation of the soul? And contrary to the myths about the period, the narrator answers in the negative, while referring to the most terrible sacrifice, the young children who died, victims who did not even get their own tombstones.

As the kibbutz pioneers and their work were held in the highest esteem, we realize that the criticism implied by the stories is a severe blow to the image of the kibbutz pioneers as a shining example of the builders of an ideal society.

If mythicization occurs mainly around the deeds, the heroism and the sacrifice of the earliest settlers and the next generation, demythicization applies to aspects connected with the ideology of the early pioneers, their approach to Judaism, and especially their interpersonal relationships. Yet there is a substantial difference in the shaping of such stories compared to stories of mythicization. There are three central characteristics in them:

1. Repeated declarations about the fact that the narrator is using testimonies of other members. The narrator presents himself as a researcher of the past who collects the details of information from the kibbutz members in order to shape the story. Thus, the narrator presents his own voice as the voice of the group as he seeks to gain legitimization for his story.

2. There is a recurring structure of expressing "the opposite voice," such as "There are those who would say . . . ," "Regarding this, there are some who maintain . . . ," and so on. The narrator presents what he anticipates or fears his audience will express, and thus may interrupt the story and turn the discourse to an argument. Thus the narrator achieves two things: he prevents involvement and an attack and enables himself to give a response to the words of "those who maintain," but he also presents himself as part of the group, as someone who is aware of the multifaceted voices within it, without giving up his own voice.

3. An undertone of apology and defense. The narrator is aware of the injury and pain his story causes and justifies his act with values having central importance in the present for the narrating society.

One of the means culture uses for demythicization is changes in genres. Yael Zerubavel has shown how the jokes about Joseph Trumpeldor have become a means for demythicization in Israeli society (1991).[14] The case in the demythicization stories told by Yair Benari is not similar. The storyteller weaves local legends about people and deeds that took place and have been forgotten or were made to be forgotten because of circumstances, because they lacked accord, because they challenged the ideology, or because they dealt with a subject too painful for the society. The story, which redeems them from oblivion, criticizes that they have been forgotten and attempts to revive these people and deeds and to present them as part of the ethos of the kibbutz settlement.

The stories of demythicization expose not only the image of the narrator, but also the image of the kibbutz society. One of the distinct characteristics of Ein Harod is its being a society that sanctifies memory. Almost from the beginnings of the existence of the kibbutz it was customary to issue memorial booklets about every member, and not only about the dominant figures as was the custom at many other kibbutzim. The early settling of Ein Harod was documented widely by its members, and its immense archive, which includes writings, documents, photographs, and more recently, recordings and film, attests to this activity.

When I started working on my research project, I did not anticipate the existence of such a large number of demythicizing stories, due to the special character of kibbutz society. Indeed such stories are not always well liked, especially by the old-timers. A kibbutz member once said to me: "I was in the old cemetery when Yair [the storyteller] was taking a group of youngsters on a guided tour, and I was shocked. Is this what he feels he must tell them about Ein Harod? That there were cases of suicide, of betrayal and things like that? Other things happened in Ein Harod, didn't they?"

Demythicization is always hard, on every society. However, there is no real objection to these stories, and it is chiefly young people who want to hear them. It would be correct to say the shattering of myths is possible in Ein Harod. Are these stories also a response to external criticism in a time of low ebb of the kibbutz in Israeli society? Although this is probably an influencing variable, it seems to me that what we have here is primarily an internal reckoning that reflects the feelings of the narrator and his audience, who come to do their own reckoning with their world, according to changing societal values. As is true with many stories of demythicization, Gellerman's story and the story about the children's graves are, in addition to the criticism and protest, also an attempt to make justice and to emphasize the contributions of those anti-heroes who did not find expression in the heroic period of the inception of the kibbutz and are thus not included in the collective memory of the kibbutz.

The kibbutz collective memory, like collective memory in any society, is a woven fabric of the personal memories and is a product of the reciprocal relationships among individuals (Connerton 1990). The weight of the various memories in forming the collective memory is not equal. The power of the elite, of course, is a dominant force. Those who were among the elite of the kibbutz during the period of establishment and growth, those who made themselves heard in public, are better kept in the memory. As he seeks to introduce a change in the collective memory, the narrator's authority lends him his status—enabling him to be heard in public. In this respect, he does not differ from the elders of the tribe who left their impression on the collective memory of the tribe as they told its history.

As mentioned, a number of times I have heard voices of protest, primarily on the part of the old-timers of the kibbutz, alleging that these stories are destructive, that they expose the weaknesses of the kibbutz and damage the fabric of collective life. It seems to me that the opposite is true. Stanley Meron has discussed the survival powers of the kibbutz in a changing society. He argues that the strength of the kibbutz derives from its adaptive powers: the kibbutz is able to adjust to social and economic changes, to the transition from agriculture to industrialized agriculture and from there to industrialization (1981). The kibbutz is a social movement that carried out a heroic revolution in the past, but the test for today's kibbutz is its ability to continue its survival. Its existence is conditioned on the will of its members and their children to continue living in the kibbutz. As early as 1973, studies of those who left the kibbutz indicate that individual freedom and understanding of the individual are of the highest importance among its youths (Ben-Raphael 1973). We can say that the narrator has a tacit and perhaps not totally conscious objective: to make the younger generation aware of the changes that have occurred on the kibbutz by the very fact that he is telling such stories, as well as to make them familiar with personalities from the kibbutz past with whom they can more easily identify. This embodies a manipulative tendency to bring the kibbutz milieu closer to the younger generation and to imbue them with an identification that will lead to a decision to remain on the kibbutz. The stories of the kibbutz by the kibbutz narrator are part of the cultural infrastructure of Ein Harod, and as such they reflect, if only partially, the shapes and colors of the picture as a whole. The stories criticize the rigidity of the kibbutz framework in its beginnings and expose unique characters and deeds that did not find expression in the past. Thus they express the wishes of the present, allowing personal expression, self-actualization, uniqueness, and even deviation. However, as the stories of mythicization show, the kibbutz did not divest itself of its values, the sanctification of the past and the appreciation of heroism and sacrifice of the founders. These function in the folk culture of the kibbutz alongside the criticism and the seeking for change.

The existence of the two trends of mythicization and demythicization reflects the tension between the wish to preserve a national and local mythology and the desire to portray the past in all its complexity. This tension characterizes the contemporary kibbutz society.

II
LEGENDS OF IMMIGRATION AND ABSORPTION

AN EXAMINATION OF HOW THE DEFINITION of "folklore" has changed from the eighteenth century to the present can explain why research was focused on particular groups and why certain questions were asked about them. Romanticism and the rise of nationalism in Europe, which stimulated the study into folklore, saw that study as mainly involving what Johann Gottfried von Herder called the "ancient national spirit." Accordingly, the group deemed most appropriate for study was the peasantry, considered to be a relatively stable group that had not yet been "spoiled" by civilization.[1] This led to the prevalent assumption that the songs and stories preserved by the peasants reflected the ancient national spirit and permitted its reconstruction.

From the mid-nineteenth century, folklore studies in England were influenced by the British anthropology of Edward Tylor, who saw evolution as a reflection of human history. Folklore studies were viewed as a historical discipline that compared and identified archaic survivals of beliefs and customs (Tylor 1871). It was still assumed that these survivals were to be found chiefly in relatively stable populations, and no one imagined that other groups might be appropriate objects of study.

The changing definition of folklore, starting with William Bascom (1953), who saw folklore as a verbal art, and continuing with Dan Ben-Amos (1975) and Robert Georges (1983), who see folklore chiefly as a communicative process of a particular type, leaves aside the element of antiquity and opens new horizons for research. It is no longer assumed that folklore exists in a situation of social stability. Hence new groups—including immigrants—become the object of study, and new questions are asked.

In examining the research model that was dominant for years in the study of the folklore of immigrants and ethnic groups in North America, Georges (1983a) demonstrates how the model was influenced by the British anthropological tradition of studying survivals, decades after this tradition ceased to be the dominant school. Folklorists continued to see themselves as engaged in a campaign to rescue folklore. Immigrant traditions were viewed as survivals that had to be documented at once, before they vanished as a result of contact with the new culture. How-

ever, as Georges shows, with the passage of time new research orientations emerged, and scholars began to focus on the process of transition
and how it modifies the folklore that the immigrants brought with them
from their countries of origin. In these studies such change is viewed
as a natural part of the transition, not as an unfortunate but inevitable development whose final outcome must necessarily be the absolute
elimination of the cultural differences between ethnic groups and the
dominant culture.[2]

In the study of immigrant and ethnic folklore in Israel, the accent
seems to have been placed chiefly on Georges's "first model." Expressions like "saving the immigrants' traditions," "rescuing what can still
be saved," "studying the folklore that is still alive," are very frequent. Although the changes in traditional folklore brought about by the transition to the new culture have also been studied (Hasan-Rokem 1982;
Bar-Itzhak and Shenhar 1993), there has been less attention to the creation of folklore as a direct result of the contact with the new place and
new culture (Schely-Newman 1991; Bar-Itzhak 1992).

With Israel's influx of mass immigrations from Asia and Africa in
the early years of statehood, a national absorption policy was elaborated, one of its chief architects being David Ben-Gurion. In Ben-Gurion's formulation, the purpose of statehood was to facilitate the cultural
absorption of the immigrants; it was to expedite the process of "blending" of the returning exiles through a set of values and symbols that
laid emphasis on what the different population groups had in common
and that hallowed the principles of national unity and state sovereignty.
This "statist" approach combined universal values rooted in socialist Zionism with a rigid concept of national unity, which was interpreted as
uniformity, and rejected the traditional customs of the various ethnic
groups and the folk culture as divisive manifestations left over from the
Diaspora (Liebman and Don-Yehiya 1983).

There were those who regarded the acquisition by the new immigrants of values developed in the *Yishuv* period as inevitable, and even
applied the term "assimilation" (Frankenstein 1951, 273–75) in concluding that there was no room for the preservation of "cultural enclaves" in
Israeli society. Some, like G. Spiegel, even asserted that the assimilation
of the members of the oriental ethnic groups (Mizrahim) into Ashkenazi Israeli culture was essential due to the absence of equality between
the cultures, "inasmuch as they have little of value to offer to modern
culture. Therefore they must abandon their demand 'to preserve their
culture and their folklore,' for they thereby foster the persistence of

alienation and divisiveness among the sections of the people" (Spiegel 1963, 147–48). However, the traditional background of the Sephardim and Mizrahim rendered difficult intercourse with them through the medium of the concepts and symbols of socialist Zionism.[3]

Ben-Gurion's rejection, which stemmed from the "Negation of the Diaspora" and was applied to all immigrant groups, was interpreted later as a denial of the culture of the Sephardim and Mizrahim by the Ashkenazim. Sammy Smooha (1978), for example, stresses the paternalist approach of the Ashkenazim to the oriental ethnic groups, which were deemed to be antiquated, backward, of limited talent, and incapable of being equal partners in the national enterprise. They were objects for help and training for a society whose Ashkenazic culture was perceived as the national Israeli culture. Smooha asserts that the cultural hegemony of the Ashkenazim, which imposed cultural unity, attenuated the cultural heritage of the Sephardi and Mizrahi immigrants and attempted to force them into conformity with the dominant Ashkenazi line. It even resulted in a situation in which they accepted the prejudices that were directed against them and so developed inferiority complexes and lost the ability to believe in themselves. The problem of the ethnic groups in Israel derives not only from the unequal allocation of resources between immigrants and veteran Israelis in the period of mass immigrant absorption in the 1950s, but also—perhaps principally—from the rejection of the cultural values that the immigrants brought with them.

Unlike official policy toward the immigrants' culture, folklorists saw it as an important field for study. The collection of immigrants' folk narratives began in the 1950s. The establishment of the Israel Folktale Archives by Dov Noy, in 1955, was an important manifestation of this attitude.

Nevertheless, as noted above, the scholarship was oriented more toward preserving and rescuing the folklore the immigrants had brought with them from their native countries and less toward studying its metamorphoses in the wake of their migration and the creation of new folklore among immigrant groups in Israel.

3

"The Camouflaged Plums": Sweet versus Bitter in Legends of Absorption of Polish Jews

The most important change in immigrant folklore studies, as I see it, is the focus on folklore created by immigrants based on their experience as immigrants. Of course the immigrants still use the well-known and familiar cultural patterns they brought from the "old country." But their new creations are an immediate outcome of their migration and everything it implies. These creations can emerge only in the wake of their migration, in a fashion that is a direct result of all the factors involved in this migration. The key contribution to this kind of study of Eastern European Jewish immigrants to North America was made by Barbara Kirshenblatt-Gimblett (1978), who associated cultural shock with the creation of folklore.

Here I would like to offer some findings of fieldwork to study whether the radical cultural change, the culture shock, experienced by immigrants who came to Israel from Poland in the late 1950s inspired them to create folklore, and, if so, the areas in which it developed, its forms, and its functions.

Historians refer to this wave of immigration as the "Gomułka aliya," after the Polish Communist leader of the period. This migration brought 42,289 Polish Jews to Israel between 1956 and 1960. Because the peak year was 1957, when 29,529 immigrants arrived, it was also known as the "1957 Aliya." The large exodus from Poland followed the change of government there in 1956. The new regime unleashed a new torrent of anti-Semitism, but also opened the gates for Jewish emigration, which had been illegal for several years. By way of characterizing the causes and motives of this wave of aliya, let me quote Hersh Smoller (as cited by Yisrael Gutman 1985), who distinguishes between this "second wave" of Polish aliya and the "first wave," who emigrated after World War II and the Kielce pogrom:

> Then [in 1945–46], many Jews who had not yet had a chance to settle down fled in panic. Many were still sitting on their suitcases. Things were different with the "second wave." Families came then who had already integrated, who had apartments, furniture, jobs, a livelihood. The children were in school, the teenagers were working or in high school. In this situation the decision to throw everything away and leave was far from easy. . . . Unlike the "first wave," after the Kielce pogrom, when masses of ordinary folk fled in confusion, the "second wave" was marked by the departure of many who had no contact with a Jewish environment, assimilated persons who frequently made a public show of their Polishness.

The fieldwork was conducted in a town that for all intents and purposes was established just to absorb this wave of immigrants—Upper Nazareth (*Natzrat Illit*). This town was founded in 1957 on a ridge in the lower Galilee, adjacent to Old Nazareth, but as a separate jurisdiction with the name Qiryat Nazereth (Nazareth). The reasons for establishing the town were related to demography and security; that is, setting up a Jewish town near an Arab urban center, with the idea that it could eventually become the capital of Galilee and northern Israel—an idea realized in 1974 when it received full municipal status.[1] As a first step, eleven families of veteran Israelis were recruited to provide the administrative infrastructure for the new community (administrators, teachers, and the like). These families first met at the site in January 1957, the same month that the initial fifteen families arrived from Poland. Month after month, more Polish immigrants arrived, along with families of veteran Israelis, in the ratio of 70 percent immigrants to 30 percent veterans.[2]

The Ministry of the Interior appointed an interministerial committee to administer Qiryat Nazereth, comprising functionaries from various government ministries and chaired by a representative of the Defense Ministry. In 1962 a local council was appointed, with representation from among the town's residents selected to reflect the proportional results of the previous year's Knesset elections. All of its members were veteran Israelis. It was not until 1965, eight years after the founding of the town, that the first local-council elections were held.

In addition to those from Poland, immigrants from Hungary and especially Romania were sent to Qiryat Nazereth. In 1960 the first wave of immigrants from North Africa—Algeria, Tunisia, and Morocco—arrived. These early arrivals were employed in industry, construction, services, and make-work projects. There were also the first stirrings of private enterprise, chiefly small grocery stores, even though most purchases were made in the markets of Arab Lower Nazareth.

The waves of immigration from Asia and Africa have been the subject of sociological studies in Israel (Eisenstadt 1967, 151–66); anthropologists, too, have preferred to focus on those groups. When I asked several sociologists why there has never been a study of the immigrants from Poland, they answered that the group had no problems and had consequently not drawn attention. One reason for gathering and examining the folklore created by these immigrants was to find out whether it could provide an answer, even if only partial, to the "nonproblematic" nature of this group, since the immigrants themselves, as we shall see, were indeed exposed to many difficult problems of integration.

When I went out to do my fieldwork, I expected to find chiefly family stories, the kind of absorption stories that are handed down in families and deal with the period of immigration and the difficulties of absorption. However, I found much more new folklore that went beyond the family circle—aphorisms, phrases, and stories with thematic similarity and formal identity shared by the entire group. These were created mainly at the interface of the traumatic encounter between the immigrants and their new reality.

The first large category of folklore dealt with the initial encounter with the physical conditions of the new country. For immigrants from Europe, the Israeli climate was hard to bear. This immediately led to "homiletical derivations" of words and names.[3] Thus *hamsin,* the name for the dry desert wind that the immigrants learned from the old-timers, was given a Polish "etymology" based on phonetic similarity: *hamsin* became *chamski syn,* Polish for "son of a hoodlum," and so they called this cruel wind.

Polish Jewish folklore was always polyglot (An-Ski 1925, 257–62; Noy 1962, 49–56; Bar-Itzhak 2001, 29). This multilingualism was preserved in the folklore of the immigrants, but with a significant change from the situation in the Diaspora. Whereas in Poland the language that served as the distinctive identifying and unifying code was Yiddish, supplemented by a few words of Hebrew (such as *amkha* to indicate that a person spoken of was a Jew), in Israel the situation was inverted. This is particularly conspicuous in the epithet the immigrants applied to their new home, Qiryat Nazereth, drawing on the tradition of homiletical derivations of names they had brought with them from the Diaspora. In their legends of origin about the earliest Jewish settlement in Poland, Polish Jews derived the name Poland from the Hebrew *Po-lin,* meaning "tarry here," because it was the place where they found rest after years of persecution and wandering. That is, the Polish word was Judaized and explained on the basis of Hebrew (Bar-Itzhak 2001, 29–32). In Israel the immigrants called their new home *Qiryat Natzorres*—"a town on troubles." The Hebrew word *Natzeret* was given the Ashkenazic pronunciation *Natzores* and was then further distorted to give it a meaning in Polish and Yiddish. In Polish, *na* means "on," while in Yiddish, *tsorres* means "troubles." The immigrants' reference to their new home as a "town on troubles" expressed the problems they encountered in their attempt to integrate.

The immigrants remember there were few buildings, and those were built of stone, an architecture unfamiliar to them. There was little greenery, and the ground was rocky. The wild landscape and even more so the unfamiliar animals were the source of great anxiety. Snakes, scorpions, lizards, and chameleons were seen as primeval creatures, known to them previously only from books. This was the background for the "monster" story that circulated among the Polish immigrants.

The following formalized description of the texts is based on the method of Vladimir Propp (1968).[4] The formal structure of the "monster" story runs as such:

1. The hero (the narrator or someone he knows) steps on an object without noticing it.
2. The "object" wakes up and turns out to be a snake, scorpion, or lizard that traps the hero (for example, in one version, the hero is entering his house, the snake was on the threshold and the hero thought it was a walking stick, but it springs into activity and blocks his way back out).
3. The trapped hero looks for a way to defend himself and lights on some object quite inappropriate for this (usually some object provided to immigrants by the Jewish Agency, such as an aluminum bucket, a broom, a stool, or a kerosene lamp).
4. The hero uses this implement to fight off the "monster" and wins the battle (he kills the animal or chases it away).

In a number of stories, there is another narrative function:

5. A veteran Israeli who happens to pass informs the hero that the animal in question was quite innocuous.

Here is one example of the "monster" story:

When we arrived, the place was utterly desolate. I sent my wife and daughter to my sister in Haifa and stayed here alone. Every afternoon I used to go out and try to plant a garden. One day I come back and cross the threshold. I saw there was a stick on the threshold, but I didn't pay any attention to it and stepped over it. No sooner had I entered the room than I see that the stick is following me—it wasn't a stick but a snake, which begin to dance in front, while blocking my path back to the door.

What could I do? There was no place to run to, and in Poland I had never had anything to do with snakes. I look around and next to me I see the bucket we had received from the Jewish Agency. In those days, when we came from Poland, I was healthy—I must have weighed around a hundred kilos. I grab the bucket, put it over the snake's head, and sit on it, and, what do you expect, my weight severed its head. I was petrified! I took the snake by the tail and ran to my upstairs neighbors, who were old-timers from Afula. They heard the story and began to roar with laughter, because the snake wasn't poisonous.[5]

What these stories expose, first of all, are the anxieties of the narrating society. But they also give them a way to vent these anxieties by the mere act of expressing them. The story is a metaphor for the condition of the immigrants, who feel that they have come to a primordial wasteland. From this perspective, the story expresses a binary opposition between nature and culture, to use the concepts of Claude Lévi-Strauss (1963, 206–31). The hero resembles a person who has gone from a civilized habitat to a place where nature lies bare and exposed, overrun by primeval monsters. Settling in an unfamiliar place, asserts Mircea Eliade, resembles an act of creation. Strange districts are associated with chaos, with pre-creation. Settlement is tantamount to converting chaos into cosmos by means of a ritual that actualizes it (1991, 9–10). The transition story is both an expression of and part of the ritualistic act.

The transition itself, represented in the stories by the crossing of the threshold, leaves the hero trapped and with no way out, his back to the wall, with monsters dancing in front of him and barring his way. This is how the immigrants conceive of their own situation. They know there is no way to return to the former situation, which, although it did not lack difficulties, was known and familiar. They know the only way out is to deal with the Israeli "monster" and to overcome it, if possible.

The hero of the story has no means appropriate for dealing with the new situation. He does not know the nature of the "monster," and the various objects provided by the Jewish Agency are not really meant for self-defense. This, of course, constitutes implicit criticism of the absorption methods themselves. Nevertheless, the hero is a doer. Instead of throwing in the towel, he takes up the unsuitable tools, because they are the only ones at hand. But in addition to them, he also applies the wealth he retains from his past—experience of life, the ability to improvise, a capacity to withstand perilous situations and survive. Indeed, despite the inappropriate implements, his readiness to act and his powers of invention lead him to victory.

Interwoven throughout the story is a vein of humor that the narrator directs at the hero, who is sometimes himself or his alter ego. The fact that an experienced adult lets himself be trapped creates the self-directed irony so typical of Eastern European Jewish humor (Noy 1962, 118–21; Oring 1992).[6] The hero's duel with a threatening "monster," armed only with an aluminum bucket or a kerosene lamp, is a genuinely comic scene. The humorous climax of some of the stories turns the entire plot into a tempest in a teapot and reflects the narrator's attitude toward himself and his peers and his ability to see the amusing side of their anxieties.

Nevertheless, even if the monster turns out to have been a totally harmless creature, in the final analysis the narrating society does not view the incident as much ado about nothing. The incident is important precisely because it highlights the trap in which the immigrant finds himself and forces him to take a stand and act. This reveals the optimism of the immigrants from Poland, who, having experienced the horrors of the Holocaust, know that you must go on, no matter what. The story also makes it clear that even though Israeli society has not provided the immigrants with the appurtenances that would facilitate their integration, he can make them do the trick if he remembers that he has other resources derived from his earlier experiences—determination, perseverance, power of invention, and the ability to get by in situations of pressure and distress. From this perspective, the story confirms the positive self-evaluation of the narrating society alongside its characteristic self-directed irony.

The food in Israel, too, was quite new. Many immigrants told of bad stomachaches during their first days in the country. The new foods became the subject of many stories. Below is a story that, based on one variant, I call "The Camouflaged Plums." The formal structure is as follows:

1. The hero (the narrator or someone he knows) is invited to a meal at the home of someone who has been in the country longer (a relative, a veteran immigrant on a kibbutz, etc.).
2. The host puts a dish of tiny plums on the table.
3. The hero is astonished by their small size and compares them in his mind with the plums he remembers from Poland.
4. The hero tastes the plums (the narrator first describes the hero's anticipation of the taste of the dearly loved fruit) and spits them out.
5. The host laughs at the hero and makes fun of him: "They're olives!" he announces.

The epilogue to these stories may be "to this day I can't eat them"; but it may also be "and today I've learned to eat and enjoy them."

Here is an example of this story:

The old-timers never stopped trying to recruit me to join the Mapai party. They organized outings to kibbutzim and persuaded me to come along. Around noon we came to the dining room, where I saw lots of tiny plums in a bowl on the table. I didn't understand why they were serving dessert before the main course and why the tour organizers were eating them even before the meal. For me, in Poland, plums were dessert. But the plums in Poland were colossal, maybe the size of apples, and so sweet. What can I tell you, throughout the meal I thought about the plums and could already taste their sweetness in my mouth. When the meal was over I took a tiny plum and popped it into my mouth. The taste was so bitter that I spat it

*out. I couldn't restrain myself. They just laughed and laughed. "What, you
didn't know they were olives?"*[7]

This story has a broad circulation among Polish Jews in Israel, far beyond Upper Nazareth. It likens the immigrant to an infant who doesn't
know what he is putting into his mouth. Here, too, we encounter the
typical humor of self-irony, a result of the description of an adult who
behaves like an infant—putting things into his mouth without knowing
what they are and then spitting them out.

The story also expresses the longings for one's native country, or at
least for familiar things. The hunger for plums expresses the immigrant's
craving for known and familiar tastes. The description of the hero an-
ticipating their flavor is comic, because the adult hero is described as a
gluttonous child. But it also expresses the immigrant hero's lack of self-
confidence, reflected by his joy when he can catch hold of something
that seems to be familiar.

The story presents two fundamental oppositions between the plums
of Poland and the supposed plums of Israel. First of all is the size—large
in Poland, small in Israel. This can be interpreted as a metaphor for the
situation of the immigrant, whose stature has become dwarfed not only
in the perceptions of the new society (which laughs at his reaction) but
also in his own eyes. The second contrast is that of sweet versus bitter.
The hero's mouth waters at the thought that he is about to taste the
sweet fruit of his native country; instead he fills his mouth with the acrid
bitterness of the Israeli fruit. This can be understood as a symbolic expression of disappointment and difficulties of absorption, which leave
an unexpected bitter taste in the immigrant's mouth. What is more, he
is not familiar with Israel and its fruits, of which the olive is one of the
most important and sacred, one of the biblical Seven Species.

Explicit laughter erupts twice in this story. The first time is within
the narrative, where the object of the laughter is the disappointed hero
who spits out the bitter fruit and those amused are the old-timers, who
know quite well what an olive is. But there is also laughter in the narrative situation. Here the narrator and his audience chuckle at the hero,
their alter ego, because in the wake of such an incident they, too, know
what an olive is. The incident in which they are portrayed as risible heroes is perceived as having been worthwhile after all, because it taught
them something, brought them closer to the new reality, and helped
them internalize it.

The Spheres of the Social Encounter

Folklore reflects tensions in the contact between immigrants and old-timers, who, as already noted, occupied all the key positions in the town, leaving the immigrants extremely dependent on them. One must remember that in Israel of the 1950s, one's seniority in the country was still a criterion for determining social status and the allocation of resources (Eisenstadt 1967, 166–82). Sometimes political pressures were exerted on immigrants by the bureaucrats of the agencies they depended on for their daily bread. At first the immigrants found hardly any arena where they could enjoy a full and equal social partnership with the old-timers. It is true that the veteran society, which saw itself as the integrating society, drilled into the immigrants the notions of full equality, solidarity, and partnership in the creative enterprise—but on the condition that the host society's existing groupings and parties were deemed suitable to all the immigrants' desires, needs, and aspirations. The underlying conception of immigrant absorption in those years, which excelled in a disposition to mold the immigrants' lives, to the greatest extent possible, to fit into the existing social orientations and values, which rejected the Diaspora, produces great tension (Liebman and Don-Yehiya 1983).[8] The immigrants felt that even what was precisely dearest to them, their own language—meaning chiefly Yiddish (even more than Polish)—was denigrated and rejected. So the immigrants called on this language to respond to the veterans tit for tat. The epithet the immigrants affixed to the old-timers was based, once again, on a verbal echo with a Yiddish word and a borrowed signification. The Hebrew word *vatiq*, "veteran" or "old-timer," became *vetig*, which means "pain." This epithet became a unifying code word for the group and demarcated its difference from the host group that perceived itself as an elite and, through the connotation attached to the word, challenged this perception. In fact, the *vetig* figures in many stories and expresses the relations between immigrants and old-timers.

The encounter with Arab society, too, was a shock. The immigrants who were brought to Qiryat Nazereth had to pass through the streets of Lower Nazareth in order to reach their new home. The encounter produced many stories of astonishment at the sight of men in dresses and headscarves. But the relations that developed between the two groups were for the most part positive.[9] The immigrants appreciated the business sense of the Arabs of Nazareth, sold them goods they had brought from Poland, traveled with Arabs in Arab buses, and were delighted to discover not only that some of the Arabs spoke Polish, having come into contact with General Władysław Anders's army during its stay in the country during World War II, but also that the Arabs were quick to learn Yiddish and did not condemn it, as the veteran Israelis did.

At the same time, there was an uneasiness about intimate relations, which stemmed precisely from the mutual attraction of east and west. The following story, which also has a broad circulation, embodies this anxiety.

1. The heroine is a woman known to be intimate with Arab men (the narrator does not refer to a specific woman but takes pains to indicate that everybody knew her).
2. The heroine is warned against continuing this unacceptable conduct.
3. The heroine pays no attention to the warnings and continues to behave this way.
4. The heroine's head is shaved in the middle of the night.
5. The mortified heroine cannot leave her house.

The narrative function of the head shavers is filled by various figures ·in different stories. Usually we are told that "nobody knows who they were," a mechanism that aligns the story with sacred legends by alluding to the intervention of celestial powers, even though most of the Polish immigrants were not religious. Sometimes they are "some of our young men," and sometimes "they were young fellows from the *shvartzes*" (in the Israeli context, this meant immigrants from North Africa), "who are hotheaded and hate Arabs."

This is a story about setting boundaries. The situation that confronted the immigrants after their arrival in Israel was one in which values and norms were blurred. Many of the values they had brought with them from their country of origin were rejected by the dominant culture. This, as we have noted, produced alienation and even hostility. Arab society, despite its differences and remoteness, did not threaten the immigrants. On the contrary, it treated them with the respect and esteem that was so conspicuously absent in the attitude of the Jewish host society. In this situation, and given the geographic proximity between Jews and Arabs, the fear developed of a type of intimacy that is forbidden by Jewish religious law and in any case seemed inappropriate to most of the immigrants.

The story attempts to set these limits clearly, casting a woman as the victim. Her punishment of having her hair cut off alludes to the many connotations of hair in Jewish tradition, while at the same time borrowing a penalty that was commonly meted out in Europe during World War II to women who were too friendly with the enemy.

This brings us to stories that express the relations between the immigrants from Poland and those from other countries. As noted above, immigrants came to Upper Nazareth from Hungary and Romania as well and later, in 1960, from North Africa.

There is evidence of a great deal of mutual segregation at first, expressed in folklore through epithets and stereotypes such as *igen-migen* for immigrants from Hungary, associated with jocular Yiddish rhymes like "We called them *Igen-mign, khap di fligen*" ("*Igen-migen,* catch the flies"). Romanian emigrants were called *Romaneshte* or *Romeiner-ganev* (Romanian thief), while *shvartze* (black) was applied to Moroccan Jews.

The Poles looked down on this last group, as reflected in the following story.

1. The hero or heroine goes to the home of new immigrants from Morocco.
2. The hero or heroine is invited to stay for dinner.
3. The hero or heroine asks to use the facilities, only to discover that the toilet bowl is being used as a crock for curing pickles!

Here is one example of this story:

Moroccans moved into the other end of the tenement house. What can I tell you—the first time I saw them, after they arrived, I thought the prophet Elijah had come to the block. They wore white dresses with a three-cornered hat and triangular white shoes. With the beard they looked just as I had always imagined Elijah the Prophet.

There was one man whom I used to greet cordially every morning and he returned the greeting. One evening, when I was coming home, he was standing outside. He took me by the hand and gestured that he wanted me to come inside with him. I didn't want to, but it wasn't nice to refuse. We went inside and he called his wife, who began to run back and forth and put food on the table, all sorts of delicacies. He pushed everything into my

*mouth. The food was spicy, but I had no choice, I had to eat it. Finally my
stomach began to hurt and I had to go to the bathroom. I went in there and
what did I see? The toilet was stuffed full of cucumbers! That's how it was
back then. They didn't know what a toilet was for.*[10]

This story, which I recently heard directed at Jews from Ethiopia (in
slightly different form), is always told in a context that turns it into an
apologetic tale, namely, why the narrator preferred to keep his distance
from this group at the time of their first encounter. One of the basic dis-
tinctions in the civilized world is that between food and excretion. The
ethnic group targeted in this story is one that according to the tale does
not distinguish the two and hence is not to be considered civilized. The
story recounts the "primitive" nature of the members of that community when they arrived in Israel and is presented to justify the attitudes
of the narrator and his or her community at that time.

A study of the folklore created by Polish Jews after they arrived in
Israel in the late 1950s can explain, even if only partially, why the absorption of this group was not problematic and why the sociologists
never studied them. However, they *did* have many problems. The shock
of the encounter with Israeli society and culture was no less strong, and
in some areas perhaps even stronger, than that experienced by other
groups of immigrants. Nevertheless, an analysis of these stories reveals
three central traits that reflect the Polish immigrants' cultural outlook:

1. Optimism, which spurs the heroes on to try to deal with any
   situation. Even when the situation seems desperate, the heroes do not throw up their hands in despair. Instead, they
   fight on bravely, even though the only weapons available are
   quite inappropriate for the task at hand;
2. A high self-esteem, even though it is not shared by the host
   society;
3. Humor—the willingness to see what is amusing and absurd
   in a situation and to laugh at themselves even in painful situations. Even the most painful situations and the fact that the
   hero is exposed to ridicule are ultimately seen as having been
   worthwhile. The hero of the story comes out the winner, because he learns from what happened to him, becomes more
   familiar with the new situation, and internalizes it.

A study of the folklore of Polish immigrants to Israel demonstrates the importance of works like this in a time of acute transition, such as immigration. Their folklore sprouted in every area where immigrants find it difficult to cope—the landscape, food, the place itself, jobs, the elites, other groups of immigrants, and Arab society. This folklore is not only an expression of the chaos experienced by any group when it settles down in a new place. It is also a means to turn this chaos into cosmos, using cultural implements from the past and adapting them to the new reality. In this way folklore serves as a means to digest the change situations, to cope with them, and to construct a bridge over them while using resources drawn from both cultures, the old and the new.

4

The Legend of Yemenite Jews
as an Expression of Immigration and Absorption

This chapter examines the folk legends of Yemenite Jews in Israel with an emphasis on the expression of the encounter with Israeli reality and culture after their immigration.[1] Needless to say, the change of language, and of country, has led to significant changes in the folk legends that the narrators brought from their country of origin, Yemen. For many of the narrators in the Diaspora, Hebrew was a language they learned only in order to be able to recite prayers and follow religious services, while in Israel they "picked up" everyday spoken Hebrew. As a result, some of the narrators, those who made the transition to narration in Hebrew, use language that is distinguished by a loss of richness as compared to their narratives in the source language, mainly with regard to rhyming and puns.[2] The new country finds expression in the imagery and metaphors used by the narrators: even modern technology creeps into the narratives.[3]

The legend is a genre of historical pretensions, or to quote Richard Dorson (1972, 160–61), these are narratives that evoke associations with well-known personages, geographical locations, and events. As distinct from the fairy tale, the legend corresponds to the real world of the narrator and his audience and is therefore accepted by them as a story they believe in (Jason 1977, 131). Hence, it is to be assumed that the legend contains representation of given problematics of the narrating society more so than other folk literary genres.

Most of the legends told by Yemenite Jews are sacred legends. Such legends deal with the central problems of the individual and society. Man faces the Sacred Power, and this power solves the problems in such a way as to maintain the stability of the sacred order. The legend, which is located within numinous-miraculous bounds, is rooted in the religious faith of the narrating society and reflects its moral-religious values. The sacred legend enables folk-religious experience, meeting people's need for a world of holiness and validating their system of folk-religious faith. A religious experience assumes the existence of a sacred world that is different in quality from the secular world. Human beings, deeds, and objects become valuable only when they take a share in the sacred world, and time, too, takes on a dimension of sacredness when the ritual is a reconstruction of events that occurred in the sacred past (Eliade 1959, 85–95).

The questions arising are: What is the picture of the spiritual-cultural existence expressed by these legends after immigration? How much do they express and represent the reality of the land of origin and the traditional values and beliefs, and in what areas does the Israeli new reality enter the stories? How is the encounter with the new reality and culture expressed in the legends, and what is the function of this representation?

The analysis of the narratives in my sample points to three major categories: (1) legends in which the plot takes place in Yemen and that concentrate on traditional themes and areas that were of importance in the land of origin; (2) legends in which the plot takes place in Yemen or both in Yemen and Israel and that deal with the annunciation of the revival of the Jewish settlement in the Land of Israel or with the establishment of the state of Israel; and (3) legends in which the plot is located in Israel and that deal with the problems in the new reality.

Category 1: Legends Set in Yemen and Concentrated on Traditional Themes

There are two main traditional themes in the first category: legends about the deeds of saintly figures (Zadikim and rabbis) and legends about the interrelationship between Jews and gentiles. The legends about the saintly figures are known in Hebrew as the Shevah legends (the "saints' legends" in international terminology). The Shevah is the narrative of a holy sanctified character (Dan 1981; Bar-Itzhak 1990). Most of the legends of Yemenite Jews that I deal with are told about Rabbi Shalom Shabazi and Rabbi Shalom Sharabi.[4] The story is set in historical time and place, and the events related, including the supernatural occurrences, are regarded as part of reality (Bar-Itzhak 1987). The Jewish Yemenite legend turns the sacred hero into an object of admiration, identification, and imitation, thereby reinforcing the conventions of holiness and fitting behavior in society. As the hero-saint is well known and close to the storytelling society, he serves as a means of religious identification for the members of the community. Shabazi, Sharabi, and other saintly figures are characterized as people who have supernatural power. The revelation of power is realized into categories: (1) sojourn with saintly supernatural characters, such as the prophet Elijah; (2) supernatural knowledge of some kind; (3) the supernatural transformation of men; (4) the supernatural transformation of space and time (e.g., Shabazi makes *Kfitzat Ha'derech* to the Land of Israel every Friday); and (5) appearance after death (cf. Bar-Itzhak 1990).

In most of the legends dealing with the interrelationship between Jews and Gentiles, the relationships are expressed through confrontation (cf. Noy 1981, 264–89). I could hardly find any folk legend that expresses harmony between the two groups.

The following legend, which has to do with both the saintly figure and confrontation, will exemplify the subject.

Once R. Shalom Shabazi was ploughing in his field. The governor of the place sent a soldier to summon the rabbi, and the soldier came to him in the field. He called out: "Ho, Jew, Jew—the governor has ordered me to take you to him. So drop your plough and leave your oxen and follow me." Shabazi did not answer the soldier and was in no hurry to run after him. He continued to concentrate on his ploughing and driving his oxen. The soldier said: "Here is a Jew like an ox who refuses to follow the furrow!"

. . .

At that instant the soldier turned into an ox. Shabazi harnessed the new ox to the plough and let one of his two oxen rest. . . .

The governor sent for Shabazi. The soldier found him in the field and ordered him to abandon his work and follow him. Shabazi ignored the soldier and his command and went on busying himself with what he was doing. "Jew, I see that you are behaving like a donkey," said the soldier. "When someone talks to you, you pretend not to understand and not to hear."

Shabazi turned the second soldier into a donkey, and harnessed him to the work and the burden. . . .

The governor sent a third soldier with instructions to bring Shabazi to him bound in ropes. This soldier swore at the saintly man and called him a dog, so Shabazi turned him into a mongrel. . . . On the fourth day Shabazi went to the governor of his own accord to find out what that evil-doer wanted with him. The governor sat on the fourth storey of his palace, and to reach him it was necessary to pass by many lackeys and to climb a great number of steps, and to request permission to pass [tablig] on every floor. Shabazi decided to take a short cut and to bypass all these obstacles. He stood by the palace and drove a peg into the ground. He struck the first blow on the peg, and the first storey of the palace sank into the ground, the storey and everything that was on it, man and beast. He struck a second blow, and the second storey sank. A third blow—and the third storey sank. The fourth storey was now level with the ground, and Shabazi could see the governor through the window and talk to him from where he was standing outside.

"What is it you require of me, sir?" Shabazi said to the wicked governor. "Why have you summoned me?"

The governor, who was secretly plotting to deal unjustly with the Jews, saw the great power of Shabazi and recanted, and abandoned the wicked plot he had intended to carry out.

He said: "The residents of the palace are screaming and yelling from the depths of the earth. Please, restore the palace to its place!"

He said: "I grant your request, on condition that you cease plotting evil against the Jews. . . ."

"And give me back my three soldiers!"

Shabazi wrenched the peg out and the palace again rose to its pristine height, and the three soldiers were their human form. . . .

May his store of good deeds stand for us and all Israel, Amen.[5]

In a way this narrative reflects Judeo-gentile interaction as seen by the narrating society. In Yemen, Judeo-gentile interaction was extremely problematic and complex. In this narrative, interaction occurs when the saint confronts the soldiers and finally the ruler himself.

Needless to say, the saint invariably gains the upper hand in all of the confrontations. The soldiers who address him using the names of animals are themselves turned into animals, and the ruler who wanted to harm the Jews is harmed by Shabazi, who causes the royal palace to sink into the ground and is then asked by the governor to raise it to the surface again. After the supernatural powers of the saint are revealed to the governor, he gives up the idea of destroying the Jews.

In this narrative the saint proves to be in possession of supernatural powers that enable him to transform Man and space. His victory over the gentiles characterizes him as a person who rescues his congregation from its persecutors, though equally as a person who establishes the superiority of Judaism to the world around it (Bar-Itzhak 1990).

The most common type of confrontation in the legends I deal with here is confrontation against the background of religion, and sometimes a socioeconomical component is added. In these narratives Jews are saved thanks to God's help or thanks to their own cleverness and even by gaining help from heroes belonging to the ten tribes living beyond the Sambation River.

In other stories of this type, confrontation against the background of religion is expressed through sexual confrontation. Here we find two categories. The most common tells that an upper-class gentile loves a Jewish girl and is even prepared to marry her. But the girl would rather die than surrender to him. The most widespread legend of this type is about Sham'a, Shalom Shabazi's daughter. The king's son wants to marry her, and the king forces Shabazi to give him his daughter; otherwise he will harm the Jews in Yemen:

Rabbi Shalom Shabazi returned home downcast and despondent. He clad his daughter in bride's dress and said to her: "My good and pure daughter, today I am leading you to your wedding." The daughter asked: "Father, who is my husband?" Her father replied: "Afterwards, daughter, afterwards you will see." He brought her to the king's courtyard, and when the king and his son came out to conduct them to their wedding, and the daughter saw who the groom was, she cried out: "Oh my father, death is preferable to me than life!" Rabbi Shalom Shabazi muttered a certain verse and the daughter fell and died in purity.[6]

In other legends a Muslim woman tries to seduce a Jewish man who is saved mostly thanks to the fulfillment of the Jewish commandments or by using his cleverness and cunning.

As stated above, all of these narratives, although being narrated in Israel, are set in Yemen and reflect the reality of the place of origin as well as the sacred values and beliefs, thus pointing to the cultural patterns of continuity of Yemenite Jews in Israel.

Category 2: The Annunciation of the Revival in the Land of Israel

The second category of legends as mentioned above take place in Yemen, or both in Yemen and Israel, and deal with the annunciation of the Jewish revival. These legends point to the fact that the Zionist nationalist revival was interpreted by Yemenite Jews as *Pa'amei Mashiah,* the coming of the Messiah, and the redemption of the people as a religious act. The legends concentrate on the way the annunciation about the revival reaches the Jews in Yemen. The legends portray the event as a vision and revelation using traditional modes of characterization that are very well known in the traditional folk narratives of Yemenite Jews as well as in apocalyptic narratives in Jewish ancient literature. The protagonist has a vision, and the annunciation is made by a sacred messenger, usually the prophet Elijah, who reveals himself most often in a dream to a righteous person (man or woman). The message is delivered through symbolic language rooted in the Jewish tradition of redemption.

In one of the legends an old man comes to a righteous rabbi and asks him to follow him:

And when they arrived to a far away place near the sea, the righteous Rabbi saw seven stars falling into the sea one after another, and from the sea a tree was raising up, high very high. The Rabbi asked the old man: "What are those falling stars?" The old man answered: "The seven falling stars are the seven Arab Kingdoms falling to the abyss."

"And what is the meaning of the tree growing from the sea?"

"The redemption comes, my son. This is the trunk of Israel that rises and grows from the sea of troubles."

The old man took the Rabbi on his back and flew with him beyond waters, mountains and hills until he brought him to Mount Carmel in the

Land of Israel, the place where the Prophet Elijah killed the Ba'al priests.

Suddenly the old man left the Rabbi near a tree and he himself entered the cave. He stayed there for a while and then returned, approached the Rabbi and asked him: "Do you know who I am?" The Rabbi answered: "I recognize you, Sir, you are the Prophet Elijah that came to announce the revival of Israel."

And indeed the Prophecy came true. Before long all the Jews in Yemen took the wandering stick in their hands and went to the city of Aden. Here the representatives of the State of Israel redeemed them from the gentile rulers.

And we came to the land of our forefathers in the State of Israel, and here we are until this very day.[7]

The concluding sentence, "And we came to the land of our forefathers in the State of Israel, and here we are until this very day," connects living in Israel today with the motives for aliya. The story makes it clear that these motives were of the traditional religious sort and quite different from those that guided the Zionist movement. It is true that the Zionist emissaries who brought the immigrants to Israel are mentioned at the end of the story. But the encounter with the emissaries is preceded by the meeting between the representative of the community, the rabbi, and the prophet Elijah, whom Jewish tradition knows as the herald of the messianic redemption. Twice Elijah announces the impending redemption to the rabbi. The first time, still in Yemen, he employs well-known Jewish symbology, here given a new interpretation. The falling stars symbolize the waning of the Arab kingdoms, while the tree that grows from the sea represents the Jewish people emerging from their sea of troubles. This message is vouchsafed to the rabbi a second time, in Israel—more precisely, on Mount Carmel, to which he flew on Elijah's back. That is, the actual flight to Israel by airplane was preceded by a supernatural flight with the harbinger of the redemption, corresponding to the apocalyptic Jewish vision. It is clear from the story that the Yemenite Jews interpreted their transport to Israel by representatives of the state in the context of the religious notion of the "footsteps of the Messiah" and the herald of the redemption.

Now let us look at another story:

"I will climb the palm tree"

Once there was a certain woman, wholly righteous. All her life she had given food to poor people and had also given them charity, anonymously, before the holidays. In this way she gave and nobody in town knew about it.

One night, she went to bed and dreamed that she saw a royal edict to the effect that all the Jews were to be massacred. Elijah the Prophet was standing next to her.

"What's this?" she asked him.

He said: "Leave this country and none of you will die."

"When will this awful thing happen?" she asked.

He did not reply.

Frightened by the dream, she woke up.

"It's only a dream," she said.

She went back to sleep and the same scene was repeated. She became very agitated and frightened.

She got out of bed, washed her face, and stood up and prayed, asking that the Tishbite come again and reveal to her when they should leave the country. She went back to sleep and the dream came to her for a third time. In her panic she seized hold of Elijah and told him, "I will not let go of you until you reveal when we should leave the country." He did not answer her, but she saw a date palm growing tall alongside the city wall. She woke up and roused her husband. He got out of bed and called the city elders, the spiritual leaders of the community. They opened the Bible and read what was written there: "I said, I will climb the palm tree [go up into the date palm] and lay hold of its branches" (Song of Songs 7:9).

"If so," they said, "we will go up in the year of 'into the palm tree.'"[8]

The elders' interpretation is based on two points that cannot be conveyed directly by translation: (1) the verb here rendered as "climb" or "go up" is *'alah*, the root of aliya, the traditional term for "going up" to the Land of Israel; (2) the numerical value of "in the date palm"—*ve'tamar*—is 642, which, in the "short-form" date notation generally used for the Hebrew calendar, corresponds to the year AM 5642=1881/2—the year of the first mass aliya of Yemenite Jews to Eretz Israel.

This story is an etiological tale to explain why the first organized immigration of Yemenite Jews to Eretz Israel took place in the year 5642. The story draws no link between this aliya and the European "First Aliya" (see page 3 of this volume), which began that same year. The Yemenite aliya is clearly associated with traditional modes of revelation and iconography. The choice of the woman as the recipient of the revelation is explained by her description as a righteous woman, someone who performs both the precepts between God and human beings and those between human beings and their fellows, by helping poor people and giving them charity anonymously. This is why she merits having Elijah appear to her. She receives the injunction to leave Yemen from the prophet Elijah, who shows her the royal decree and instructs the Jews to leave Yemen. Dream revelations like hers are common both in ancient Jewish literature and in the folk narratives of Yemenite Jewry.

As in the previous story, here too the message is conveyed by a symbol—in this case a date palm. The elders interpret it in the light of a verse from the Song of Songs, the biblical book traditionally read as a celebration of the love between God and the Jewish people. The year for their aliya is derived using the ancient Jewish practice of numerology.

Here too it is clear that the Yemenite Jews viewed their return to Eretz Israel through distinctly religious lenses. Both stories indicate that the narrating society sought to explain and justify the aliya by drawing on the world of sacred values, ancient symbols, and the Bible to provide religious sanction for their migration to a state whose foundation is incompatible with the messianic myth.

Category 3: Problems of Immigration and Absorption

Legends in the third category are set in Israel and reveal problems of the storytelling society that arose as a result of the meeting with Israeli reality and culture.

Researchers from various academic disciplines have studied the problematics generated as a result of the encounter of Yemenite Jews with Israeli reality. The hardships of everyday life, the experience of the dominant Israeli culture, and the cultures of other ethnic groups have affected the society structure and the system of beliefs and opinions of the community.[9]

For the immigrants from Yemen, as well as for other immigrants, the encounter in many ways implied culture shock in the sense used by Barbara Kirshenblatt-Gimblett (1978, 109–21).[10] Yehuda Amir (1990, 63–72) quotes a letter dating back to 1937, written by a Yemenite Jew, Rabbi Israel Levy, a year after his arrival in Israel. The letter is a fascinating ethnographic document. The following passage gives expression to the encounter with Israeli reality:

> Now I am going to tell you what the Jews in Israel are like. First of all, they all shave off their beards, you won't find even one in a hundred who has a beard. All of them wear their hair long. That is the custom in Israel. Even we have adopted their custom. And all the women wear short pants, and some don't cover their heads, nobody has the right to reprimand (anyone), everybody does as he likes. And there are people who desecrate the Sabbath, and people who eat pork, everything is permitted in Israel, everybody does as he likes." (Ibid., 71)

I contend that for Yemenite Jews the folk legend constituted a traditional vehicle serving to express culture shock; at the same time, it served as a coping tool. The folk narrative is a traditional art better suited than other traditional mechanisms to give expression to, and verbalization of, the new problematics, because it is art form that is not bound by written norms, being, conversely, open to change. Folk narratives are constantly being recreated. The folk narrator creates, using familiar, well-known basic patterns; as he narrates he reshapes and reworks the traditional pattern to suit his own needs and the needs of his audience. Thanks to this openness there is not only the traditional basic structure, but also a dynamics that is absorbed by this basic structure, exhibiting the new problematics facing the narrating society.

There are three main points of friction expressed in these legends. The first involves confrontation between the generations within the ethnic group. These narratives reveal the gap between the generations that occurred in Israeli reality. Let us consider one narrative.

There was a Yemenite woman in Jaffa who received a sacred amulet in her inheritance from her mother, and her mother—from her grandmother. In the family, they guarded the amulet as something sacred and precious that cures and saves from trouble and disaster, because it was prepared by Rabbi Shalom Sharabi himself, may he be well remembered.

This woman, the owner of the amulet, had only one son, and from the moment of his birth, he had worn the amulet day and night. The mother was very pleased that the amulet was always with him protecting him from all evil.

When he grew up, the son began to object to always having to wear the amulet and he would disobey his mother and shout: "I do not believe in amulets!"

The son's words greatly saddened the mother. But despite all that she said to him, asked him, and begged him, he kept his opinion, "I do not believe."

From sorrow, the mother became sick and died.

In the son's heart, a great sorrow began to take hold. The regret and pangs of conscience didn't let him rest, and he suffered greatly from not having carried out his mother's wishes. From then on he would always wear the amulet over his heart.

Also in the war for independence, when he went out to battle, he wore the amulet over his heart in order to fulfill his mother's request.

And here in the battle, he was hit by a bullet. But it hit the amulet, and so he was saved from death, and it was as though he was born again.

All of this happened thanks to the sacred amulet of Rabbi Shalom Sharabi.[11]

The holy character in this legend is Rabbi Shalom Sharabi, who acts through one of his objects, an amulet. These narratives are usually placed within the category of narratives telling what happened after the saint had passed on, as was exhaustively shown by Dov Noy (1967).[12] A large number of such narratives were recorded from Yemenite Jews. The locale for the events is Yemen, and the amulet saves the protagonist from illness or death.

However, the locale for the events and the work of the amulet in this narrative have been moved to a new environment—Israel before and during the War of Independence. The problematics raised in the narrative are new as well, there being nothing of the kind in the traditional narratives dating back to pre-immigration times; it is connected with the change in the system of values and beliefs of the younger generation as compared with the parents' generation.

In the narrative, the mother uses the holy amulet, which is believed to have special power and which was an heirloom handed down from one generation to the next: "who received a sacred amulet in her inheritance from her mother, and her mother—from her grandmother" to protect her son. The fact that the son is an only child implies that the mother was barren or that any other children born to the family had died. Obviously, this adds to the power of the holy amulet of Rabbi Shalom Sharabi, who watched over the son's life.[13]

As long as the son was little, the mother had the power of protecting her son by means of the amulet, which symbolizes her system of values and beliefs as well as that of her generation. The removal of the amulet by the son as an adolescent constitutes the basis for the confrontation between the son and his mother, but it equally symbolizes the rejection of the older generation's system of values and beliefs, which finds expression in the twice-repeated utterance: "I do not believe in amulets."

On the plot level this brings destruction upon the mother, the representative of the older generation: "From sorrow, the mother became sick and died." This is the kind of exaggeration characteristic of the folk narrative, but in our context it lends itself to metaphoric-symbolic interpretation: when the younger generation does not relate to the spiritual life of the parents, this is tantamount to the termination of their physical life, which is felt to be devoid of meaning.

As a result of the family confrontation the son accepts his parents' way of life, although he does not share their beliefs. He starts wearing the amulet again, in memory of his mother. And now this very amulet, which protected him when he was a child, saves his life in the War of Independence. For the narrating society the holy character continues functioning in the new reality, in the environment of war in Israel, in the traditional, familiar role of savior and guardian. But a societal-cultural message is embedded in the deeper levels of the narrative: the attack on the spiritual existence of the parents undermines not only the latter's physical existence, but that of the sons as well. Only the return to, and respect for, traditional values will safeguard the continued existence of the younger generation.

Here, then, is an example of the dynamics of the legend of Yemenite Jews in Israel, which is also part of the dynamics of folk literature in general. Being orally transmitted, it is open to change and equipped to assimilate the new problematics of the narrating society. The patterns of the genre are the cultural vehicle enabling people to cope with the new reality while using their traditional tools. Moreover, the process ensures the survival and continued existence of the genre, with the raw, on-the-ground experience of the new country supplying the ingredients that are so important for its continued existence.

The second main point of friction in these legends is confrontation with the Ashkenazi culture. This confrontation is expressed as a confrontation between two representatives of the different cultures. The Ashkenazi Jew is always characterized as "the other." Let us consider one example:

One day I did not feel well, my hands and my feet hurt. My brother-in-law came and said: "Go to Natanya and see Rabbi Shalom Shabazi. Go ahead, give it a try and see for yourself, he is a Zadik and he will help you."[14]

Don't ask questions, I really went to Natanya, and there they told me: Shabazi told Bashari to construct a synagogue in a certain place, and in that place there was a certain Ashkenazi who had a refreshment stand, and he would not budge.[15] *Bashari asked him once, he asked him twice, and he asked him for the third time. He refused—"I am not going to give up this place. It's mine," he said.*

That very night, Bashari dreamt Rabbi Shabazi. He dreamt him in the night. He said to him: "Don't you speak to him, to the Ashkenazi, and don't you be bothered with him. I will get him to move out."

He appeared to him (to the Ashkenazi) at night, and did what he did, and said: "Leave that place. It's not yours. Leave it." He repeated this for several nights.

In the morning, the Ashkenazi spoke to Bashari. He said: "Shalom, come and take that place of yours. I don't want any money or compensation, I don't want anything. I dreamt at night that an old man came and I almost choked. Come and take what is yours, I don't want it."

Bashari did so, and built Rabbi Shabazi's synagogue.[16]

The narrative opens in the first-person singular and deals with the ailments of the narrator, who is told she should make a pilgrimage to the synagogue in Natanya. However, this is merely the introduction to the narrative, and the narrator tells the tale in order to explain why she visited the town and how she learned the story of the origins of the synagogue.

The narrative itself belongs to the Jewish oikotype "Desecration punished" (Aarne and Thompson '771 IFA). The Israel Folktale Archives have many narratives narrated by Yemenite Jews and members of other Jewish ethnic groups originating from Muslim countries that focus on a Muslim (generally a ruler, but sometimes just any common Muslim) who offends the saint either on the concrete level, by attempting to destroy his tomb, or spiritually, by disobeying his wishes and doubting his powers. In these narrative plots the saint or his emissaries appear at night and beat or try to strangle the Muslim. When the Muslim begs for mercy, he is told he must repent. He does so and bows to the superiority of Jewish saints. Thus, for instance, the following tale relates that a king of Yemen persecuted the Jews:

On the first day, Rabbi Shmuel did what he did, asked for God's help, and lo and behold! After nightfall they brought the king of Yemen where they brought him, and beat him up all night.

In the morning, the king of Yemen rose and told none of his friends. When they served him coffee, they found him sprawling all over his bed like a log. They asked: "What happened?" And he said: "Nothing."

The same thing happened the following evening, and again the third evening. The king could no longer keep the matter secret, and sent for his deputies and his ministers, and said to them: "They beat me up every night. Now I want you to tell me what to do."

His ministers said: "We will put guards all around the palace. If someone tries to get in, they will put him to death."

The guards were standing there, surrounding the palace, and again the Rabbi brought in the king, with God's help, and again they beat him up. The king said to his deputies: "What happened the night before happened again tonight."

What did they do? They killed the guards and appointed other guards to guard the king. And the same thing happened over again, and again, and the guards swore: "Not even a fly got in."

They realized that there was a reason for all this. What was to be done?

The ministers said to the king: "When they come for you again, tell them: "What crime have I committed? What wrong have I done?" He did so. The moment they started hitting him he said: "I want a trial! What crime have I committed, what wrong have I done?"

The Rabbi said to him: "Your guilt is great. Why do you hate the Jews living in your country, harass them, confiscate their property, rob them, ignore them and do not protect them? Now, if you promise you will respect the Jews, starting today, and treat them as equals—fine. If you don't, you will get beaten up again, you and your deputies and ministers."

The king of Yemen did some thinking, and decided to accept the conditions of the Rabbi. (IFA 11281)

The narrative follows the same traditional pattern, and the person resisting the saint's command is punished at night and almost chokes to death. The fact that the Ashkenazi in Israel fulfills the narrative role that the Muslim fulfills in the traditional legends is significant. The oikotype "Desecration punishment," as narrated by Yemenite Jews and by other Jewish communities, was the expression of the wish to stand up to the ruling Muslim majority, at least for a brief time, and to make them realize the power of Jewish saints. In Israel the change of characters expresses the relations between the ethnic groups as seen by the narrating society. In Israel the "other" is the Ashkenazi. He is, moreover, the representative of the dominant culture, a culture that, at least for a certain period of time, tended to reject and dismiss the culture of the Yemenite Jews. As early as 1936 the author of the above-mentioned letter writes: "And all this cleverness came from—the Ashkenazis. And about us, the Yemenites, to ourselves we seemed like grasshoppers and also to them we seem to be because of our poverty. First of all we do not study and we do not write and we do not know foreign languages. We can only work with God's help. But the Ashkenazis are generally rich people, they stay at school and study for fifteen or twenty years, boys and girls. You won't ever find an Ashkenazi who cannot write—either man or woman. And when they finish studying, everyone of them makes a living from his knowledge" (Amir 1990, 70). It is not surprising that in such reality the narrative role of the antagonist that the Muslim fulfills in traditional narratives is now fulfilled by the Ashkenazi who must be taught a lesson about the power of the saintly figures of Yemenite Jews.

The third main point of friction is revealed in legends that become a means toward changing the new reality and adapting it to the needs and beliefs of the storytelling community. Here we find mostly legends about the establishment of new synagogues. The synagogues are established because a saintly figure appeared in a dream, ordered the dreamer to build the synagogue, and to name it after the saint. These narratives not only legitimize the act of creating special synagogues of the ethnic group, but also lead to the renewal of old customs. For example, in many of the legends belonging to the first group the character of Rabbi Shalom Shabazi acts as a savior, deliverer, and redeemer. The events usually occur after his death, and the locale is his tomb in the town of Ta'ez, where the people made pilgrimages in order to ask for a cure for infertility or illness.[17] In Israeli reality the custom of going on a pilgrimage to Shalom Shabazi's tomb is no longer possible. But the need to follow the custom still exists among the Yemenite Jews. In order to examine the process that occurs as a result of this situation, let us consider the following narrative.

This story, I heard from the wife of Shalom Bashari, who is the owner of the synagogue of Rabbi Shalom Shabazi in Natanya.

When I went to the synagogue of Rabbi Shalom Shabazi, may his memory be blessed, Shalom Bashari's wife said to me: "Look, this is the Tora scroll of the saint. We were in Aden on the way to the Land of Israel. He, may he rest in peace, came to my husband in a dream and said to him, "Take this Tora scroll and guard it until I tell you what to do."

And they stayed in Aden for a while. Shalom took the Tora scroll and guarded it, and then they traveled from place to place, from place to place, from place to place with Shalom guarding the Tora scroll and waiting for him to appear in a dream.

And so it was until they arrived in Natanya. Here they bought some land, built a house. And then he came to him.

"Shalom, where is the Tora scroll I gave you in Aden?"

He said, "I am guarding it. And who are you?"

He said to him, "I am Shalom Shabazi. Do not let the Tora scroll out of your sight and build me a synagogue and build an ezrat nashim *[segregated women's seating area] and build a* mikvah *[ritual bath] and you will be in charge of this synagogue in my name. And my Tora scroll will be there."*

So he did.

That was the dream, and this is Rabbi Shalom Shabazi's Tora scroll.[18]

Again, the narrative centers on an object owned by the saint—Rabbi Shalom Shabazi's Tora scroll, which was given to the protagonist, who had to take it to the new home of the community; later on this Tora scroll would be the reason for the construction of a synagogue named after the saint.

The relocation of the Tora scroll was achieved by the traditional familiar device employed by the Yemenite Jewish legend, that is, the dream: the Rabbi appears to the protagonist in his sleep and entrusts him with the task of taking the Tora scroll to Israel.

The miraculous delivery of the Tora scroll, the presence of the saint, and the instructions given by him serve to create a new reality in Israel. The synagogue is turned into a place of legitimate pilgrimage, a substitute for the tomb, because it is no longer possible to make the pilgrimage to the city of Ta'ez in Yemen. We notice the lasting, two-way connection between the saints' legend and the Israeli reality. The legend acts to justify a change in the reality of Israel, both the spatial reality (construction of a synagogue) and the cultural reality (return to the old pattern of making pilgrimages and appointing localities sacred to the community). It is, of course, possible to observe a circular pattern: the wish of the community members to change reality is reinforced by the saints' legend, which is a powerful traditional tool of wide distribution.

Let us consider another narrative that shows clearly that the Rabbi Shalom Shabazi synagogue serves as a substitute for the rabbi's tomb in the town of Ta'ez.

Before we came to the Land [Israel], I took on a vow about my son Shalom, to go to Rabbi Shalom Shabazi [to go on a pilgrimage to his tomb]. And so we started out for the Land of Israel. I said, "Good, I'll take Shalom and we'll stop there on the way." And we were traveling by foot with donkeys, with horses, with children and we didn't have a chance to stop there on the way. We came to Aden and there we had to wait and wait, and I said to myself: "Why should I stop there now, with God's help we'll get to the Land of Israel and whatever will be, will be."

We went there, Shalom married and went five years without a child. He went to doctors. He went to this one; he went to that one; it didn't help.

Then I said: "Shalom, did you know that we have on us a vow to visit Shabazi [his tomb]?"

He said: "Since when?"

I said: "Since the time we were in Yemen, since you were a boy of ten years old."

I said: "Let's go to Rabbi Shalom, to Natanya [to the synagogue named for Shabazi]."

He said: "Okay mother, I'll come."

We got to Natanya, we went into the synagogue to visit the Tora scroll of Shabazi.

I said to my son: "Shalom, look, they come from Jerusalem to Shabazi, they come from everywhere and ask for his help, to have a child, to have good health. Go up to the Tora scroll."

He opened the holy ark; he prayed.

I said to him: "Shalom, go in to the Rabbi [of the synagogue], he will check in the Book for you, maybe with God's help you will have a child."

And he says: "Mother, listen, I believe in Morri Salem [Rabbi Shalom Shabazi] and in God and, with God willing, there's no need to go in to the Rabbi."

He vowed to the Tora scroll that he would give money, and we went home.

After a year, his wife gave birth to Dori, and after that she gave birth to one after another.

We believed in our hearts that this is sacred. A visit is a visit. A vow is vow.[19]

The opening passage of the narrative traces the wanderings of the narrator on her way to Israel. Due to the hardships of immigration she was unable to keep her vow and make the pilgrimage to the tomb of Rabbi Shalom Shabazi. That she had vowed to make the pilgrimage with her son, as well as the son's name, suggests that earlier she had been unable to have children. The narrator had been unable to keep her vow not only because of the hardships of the journey, but also because she decided that going to Israel would somehow substitute for the fulfillment of the vow: "Why should I stop there now, with God's help we'll get to the Land of Israel." Needless to say, for the Yemenite Jews the Land of Israel was the most holy place. But there was the additional perception of a link between Israel and the tomb of the rabbi in Ta'ez. There are several narratives about Rabbi Shabazi that mention a secret road leading from the tomb to Israel (e.g., IFA 4527). In the traditional narratives the two spaces are linked in an attempt to add a dimension of holiness to the tomb of the rabbi. The narrative plot in the story above indicates that Israel, with all its troubles and bitterness—of which the immigrants certainly had their share—is no longer the same holy country as it was in the past. The narrating society, which is in need of a holy place associated with tradition, created a holy enclave linked to the saint, even though his tomb has remained in Ta'ez.

The narrator reports that people from all over Israel who seek a cure for their illnesses make the pilgrimage to the synagogue where the Tora scroll of Rabbi Shalom Shabazi is now kept. Moreover, the narrative plot interprets the son's infertility as the punishment for the mother's failure to keep her vow, while his cure results from the visit to the synagogue. Obviously, the synagogue in the new country has replaced the tomb back in Yemen, the old country. Now the plots of saints' legends and the miracles narrated can be linked to the synagogue in Natanya, just as the plots of legends narrated in the past were linked to life in the old country.

The narrative structure is that of personal narative.[20] Over time, the narrative may undergo anonymization; then it will deal with a woman who was punished because she did not keep her vow, similar to the narrative presented above ("a certain woman from Jaffa") about the holy amulet of Rabbi Shalom Sharabi.

Eyal Ben-Ari and Yoram Bilu have discussed the sanctification of space in the development towns of Israel settled by Jews from North Africa (1981, 243–71). The sanctification finds expression chiefly in the construction of tombs for Moroccan rabbis who were buried in their country of origin but reinterred when the community settled in Israel. The Jews of Yemen do not build tombs in Israel for the saints of their community, but locales such as the Rabbi Shalom Shabazi synagogue in Natanya serve the same purpose. They express the way Yemenite Jews cope with Israeli reality: they try to change and adapt it to their needs, using familiar, well-known traditional tools.

Although Ben-Ari and Bilu note that the construction of tombs was instrumental in the preservation and revitalization of the rites connected with them, they make no mention of the genre of North African Jewish saints' legends. I have tried to show that the legend of the Jews of Yemen is a traditional cultural pattern to which the narrators attach stories taken from life in Israel after immigration. As we study the legends, we get an overview of the cultural consciousness of the narrating society while learning which coping strategies were adopted in order to deal with the new problems arising in Israel. The narratives mentioned in this chapter reveal the link between the legends and rites and customs. The narratives in which the Shalom Shabazi synagogue figures turn the house of worship into a holy place, and the pilgrimages supply the material from which the narratives are made up. The legends therefore serve as a tool for the sanctification of an ancient heritage in a new context.

The folk legend is thus illustrated for us as a dynamic text that is constantly undergoing transformation according to the needs of the storytelling society. It adapts to the social and cultural circumstances of the Yemenite Jews in Israel and serves to express the distress and the needs after their immigration, using tools and patterns deriving from the cultural framework of the past.

III
ETHNIC FOLKLORE IN ISRAEL

IN ISRAEL, A COUNTRY CREATED to absorb Jews from all over the world ("the ingathering of the exiles"), the society that ultimately coalesced was made up of diverse Jewish ethnic communities, in addition to the non-Jewish groups (which are not considered here). As immigration continued—notably during the period of mass aliya during the first decade after independence, when immigrants arrived mainly from Asia, North Africa, and Eastern Europe[1]—the number of different ethnic groups increased. More recently, Israel has absorbed two major waves of immigration, from the former Soviet Union and from Ethiopia.[2]

Ethnic identity in Israel differs from what Jews knew in the past. In Israel they experience their ethnic identity as Jews among Jews, which is quite unlike the ethnic identity of Jews among non-Jews in the Diaspora. As I have already noted with reference to the immigrants' folklore, Zionist ideology aspired to eradicate the cultures they brought with them from their original homes and to fuse the various diasporas into one Israeli collective. Members of the various ethnic groups, too, were strongly aware of the element that all the different communities had in common: religion and nationality were considered to be overriding.

Nevertheless, we should remember that each ethnic group also brought unique traditions from its country of origin. Some of these traditions, such as liturgical melodies, are associated with religion; but most of them are folklore materials that are not of a distinctively religious nature. The folk narratives the immigrants brought from their countries of origin are a central component of this folklore. The Israel Folktale Archives currently contain some twenty-three thousand folk tales, classified by their narrator's country of origin.

This ethnic folklore is always associated with the traditions the immigrants brought with them, but its development has been directly influenced by the encounter with the Israeli milieu. The immigrants rely on the folklore genres and the set of concepts and symbols derived from their original homes to cope with their new environment during their initial phase in Israel; but these genres and concepts are themselves transformed by this encounter. Thus ethnic folklore is transmuted in ways that leave it quite different from that of the country of origin. These metamorphoses are shaped by diverse factors, including how long the immigrants have been in the new country, the attitude of the host culture, the nature of their absorption, where they live, relations between the generations, and so on.

The less time an ethnic community has been in Israel, the more unique and distinctive its folklore. Language is the key element in these tales. Initially both narrators and their audiences are fluent in the language of their previous homes (the Jewish or non-Jewish vernacular they spoke back there) and the folk narratives are told in this language. The longer a community has lived in Israel, the more changes we see. In the first stage the story is still told in the mother tongue, but it is peppered with contemporary Hebrew words, alongside the classical Hebrew words that were part of the vocabulary of the Jewish languages (Bar-Itzhak and Shenhar 1993, 15–16). Later, especially after new generations are born and grow up, even elderly narrators tend to tell their stories in Hebrew, to the extent of their ability, so that their grandchildren will be able to understand them (Hasan-Rokem 1982, 129–37)—although they still prefer their mother tongue and keep observing that the story works better in that language. Even then, however, ethnic folklore retains a linguistic hallmark—the narrators' accent, how they use Hebrew, and chiefly the interpolation throughout the story of words from the home country, sometimes only names and titles, but often "minor" folk genres like sayings and parables (Alexander-Frizer 1999, 52).

The audience is a central element in the definition of ethnic folklore. Even when the story is told in Hebrew to an audience of the affinity group, the words in the mother tongue that are interspersed throughout the story arouse a whole set of connotations and emotions that do not exist for listeners who are not part of that community. When this happens we witness the power of folk narratives to express an ethnic identity even when the story is told primarily in Hebrew (ibid., 53).

In all ethnic groups, the traditional storytelling milieu was the family circle; chiefly among Sephardi, Asian, and North African Jews, it extended to the synagogue as well. Because synagogues whose worshipers all come from a specific ethnic community are a salient phenomenon in Israel, this kind of performance survives today as well. Narration in the family circle also continues to take place. But the longer the family has lived in Israel, the more likely it is to include in-laws with different origins. Ethnic folklore, including folktales, still exists even in these cases. For most members of the family the stories express their ethnic identity, because the narrators frequently recall earlier performances when they themselves heard the story, such as "my father used to relate that . . ." and because of the intense emotional experience that stimulates identification with the ethnic group. After hearing the stories, descendants of other ethnic communities who have married into the family sometimes identify with their adopted group. Others, though, reported a feeling of alienation, when, for example, they must ask for an explanation of things that are clear to the rest of them.

The request for an explanation can serve to strengthen the bond with the family and increase the questioner's involvement with its culture; but not always. Sometimes the family replies that these matters are difficult to explain or cannot be explained at all. This creates a pattern of noninvolvement that intensifies the in-law's feeling of otherness. There are those who, for various reasons, never ask questions or try to understand. In their case the ethnic narrative, remaining in part a mystery, intensifies their sense of being an outsider.

The world of the story—the values and norms it embodies, the description of customs and beliefs, the references to characters, places, and bygone times—may also express ethnic folklore. In this context folk narratives are educational: thanks to the identification with the mainly artistic experience that the story evokes, the audience learns to identify with the world represented in it.

If we examine all the various aspects of the performance of folk narratives and analyze the world of the story, we see that ethnicity is carried by individuals for whom the artistic medium of folk narrative constitutes an ongoing emotional bond to their native culture.

Part 3 of this text considers the folk narratives of Moroccan Jewry as an example of ethnic folklore in Israel. More than two hundred thousand Jews immigrated to Israel from Morocco, starting in the mid-1950s. During the 1980s, when the tales to be discussed here were recorded, more than four hundred thousand Israelis were Moroccan immigrants or their offspring; they constituted the largest single group of Israelis of Middle Eastern and North African origin. They were prominent as a distinctive group mainly in the so-called development towns and moshavim of the periphery, founded when they immigrated, and less so in the large heterogeneous urban centers. Starting in the late 1950s and throughout the 1960s, the prevalent image of Moroccans in Israel was strongly negative. They were frequently described as having failed to adapt, as having gone through communal and family crises, and as prone to violence. Scholarly studies "confirmed" parts of this stereotype (Shoham and Rahav 1967; Shtal 1979). Anthropologists detected different patterns, however. Shalva Weil found that children from Morocco evinced greater satisfaction with the family's way of life than did the children of other oriental Jewish communities (1983). Moshe Shokeid pointed out that in contrast to the stereotype that Moroccan immigrant families were ripped asunder, the family tended to preserve its role as the focus of emotional bonds; in fact, Moroccan Jewry passed on to the next generation a deep sense of family loyalty and commitment to relatives. In Shokeid's opinion, the Moroccan immigrants exemplify the continuity of strong family ties that were not weakened by the travails of aliya and the pressures of the melting-pot ideology (1987, 11–12). Chapter 5 discusses how elderly women (80–90) adapt the traditional genre of the wonder tale to the new situation, to resolve confrontational situations or to guarantee their honored status in the family that is experiencing change processes.

Finally, chapter 6 looks at how the body language of the Moroccan Jewish saints' legend expresses the ethnic identity of both narrators and listeners.

5

Old Jewish Moroccan Women
Relate in an Israeli Context

The two stories and two storytelling events in this chapter were recorded in the town of Shelomi in the 1980s. Shelomi lies in the western Galilee, not far from the Lebanese border, about twelve kilometers from Nahariya and forty-two kilometers from Haifa. Founded in the 1950s to absorb immigrants from the mass waves that followed the establishment of Israel, Shelomi is named for the father of Achihud, the leader of the tribe of Asher, in whose territory it lies. The first residents of Shelomi were immigrants from Yemen and Yugoslavia who lived in the *ma'abara* (transit camp) set up at the site. Because of the harsh conditions that prevailed, however, all of them abandoned the site and moved elsewhere. Immigrants from North Africa replaced them. At the time of my fieldwork, most of Shelomi's twenty-five hundred residents were of Moroccan origin.[1] In recent years, new immigrants from the former Soviet Union and Ethiopia, too, have settled in Shelomi.

The stories to be considered here were told by women who were past the age of eighty.[2] They told them in the houses where they lived with younger members of their families. In their country of origin, home was the natural setting in which women told stories. The stories and their underlying messages were evidently intended for the family, even though on two occasions the presence of the researcher or researchers proved significant for the creation of the storytelling event.

The stories were recounted in Judeo-Arabic, the vernacular of Moroccan Jews in Morocco, which incorporates classical Hebrew words. The narrators also interpolated words from modern Israeli Hebrew and their new geographical location, including place names (Nahariya), concepts (moshav), and the like.

Shelomi, 1992 (Courtesy of Israel Folktale Archives)

Generically, these two stories are wonder tales. The first story, told by narrator Haviva Dayan, is a mixed genre, combining the novella and the wonder tale, the latter generally considered to be a woman's genre. As I have shown previously, it was the most common genre among Moroccan immigrant women; the novella, too, was commonly told by women (Bar-Itzhak and Shenhar 1993, 16–19).

Taking all of this into account, one may argue that folk narrative, as performed by those women in the emerging ethnic folklore of Israel, expresses patterns of continuity (language, genre, place of performance), as might indeed be expected of the narratives of elderly women who are the bearers of the culture of the past.

Nevertheless, the stories and situations in which they were told are evidently a reaction to new situations and to the narrator's encounter with a new culture. They show how old women, the bearers of the traditions of the past, express the ethnic community's beliefs and opinions in a changing world and fight for their place in the family in a situation where it is the young people who adapt quickly, thereby marginalizing the older generation. All of this is done using the familiar gift that old women have possessed since time immemorial—the folk narrative.

"Old Women Are Good and They Say Sweet Things": The Mother Alaguz Tales of Haviva Dayan

The Mother Alaguz stories were told by Haviva Dayan, who was about eighty years old at the time we recorded her tales. Haviva Dayan possessed a rich repertoire of folktales, most of them wonder tales and most of which she had heard from relatives, especially her mother, back in Morocco. She reported that the stories were told at home in various day-to-day circumstances, but also on ceremonial occasions, mainly those involving women. She noted in particular the ritual to protect a newborn, which began as soon as an infant was born and continued for seven days and seven nights, until the circumcision. The ceremony was conducted in the new mother's house by women; according to Dayan, they used to tell many stories during the course of those seven days.

Haviva Dayan was a rare individual. Despite her advanced age, she remained alert and active. Perhaps the circumstances of her life had perfected these traits. Her husband had died at a relatively young age, leaving her with a house full of small children, the youngest only three months old. As the head of the family she was responsible for raising the children and supporting the family by accepting whatever work she could find, mainly sewing.

Haviva Dayan immigrated to Israel in 1964. She and her family settled initially in Massua, near Hartuv, later in Noam, and finally reached Shelomi. Particularly sad is that of the thirteen children she bore, only three were still alive when we met her. Despite her many years in Israel, she had never learned Hebrew and spoke with her family in Judeo-Arabic, the language of Moroccan Jews in their country of origin.

When the stories were recorded Haviva Dayan was living with her son Asher, the head of the Shelomi local council, and his family. At the time, it was normal for elderly Moroccan immigrant women to live with their sons or daughters, continuing the pattern that had prevailed in Morocco, where married sons usually maintained a single household with their parents (Shokeid 1987, 9). This pattern was also compatible with anthropological studies about Moroccan Jews in Israel, which found they transmitted a deep sense of family loyalty and commitment toward relatives (12).

In Morocco, elderly women exerted strong authority when it came to the home and raising the children. This authority was associated with the vast experience they had accumulated during their lives, which they

Haviva Dayan (Courtesy of Israel Folktale Archives)

shared with their family members and especially daughters, serving as an inexhaustible source of knowledge and common sense.

The changes experienced by Moroccan immigrant families in Israel influenced this authority and source of knowledge, too. It is true that the move to Israel led to a clear improvement in the status of women. In the traditional society of Morocco women were excluded from many spheres of activity outside the home, which were the exclusive province of the men. In Israel the absorption institutions treated women as equal to men; some of the absorption agents were themselves women. The Compulsory Education Law applied to both boys and girls. Women held paying jobs outside the home in agriculture, industry, and services. Sometimes they adjusted to their new lives better than the men did (Shokeid 1987, 14).

All of this is relevant for younger women and girls. The older women, by contrast, never managed to learn Hebrew, leaving them totally dependent on younger members of the family in every matter past their front door. Technological innovations left much of their traditional knowledge outmoded. For example, in one family I witnessed a dispute between the daughters and their grandmother about buying a washing machine. The grandmother was absolutely opposed, arguing that the clothes could never be as clean using the machine as when washed by hand. The younger women appeased her by saying should that prove the case, the grandmother would have to advise the daughters about washing everything again by hand. In this case the women identified the source of opposition—their grandmother's fear of losing her status in the management of the household—but rather than use this as a bargaining chip, they promised that her status would be preserved even after modern technology entered the house.

One source of elderly women's honored status was their role as storytellers. Folk narratives were a hallmark of Jewish life in Morocco. Preachers told them in the synagogue; men used them to transmit sacred values and norms as well as for entertainment. For women, the folktale was a way to educate and amuse the children. It also served to express the tensions, fears, and latent desires of women in a patriarchal society.

The Israeli milieu threatened the old women's role as storytellers. Television became the focus of entertainment. As one of the narrators told me, she no longer told stories in the evenings, as she had in the past, because everyone watched television. Most of the women in Shelomi said they told fewer stories than in the past and their families were less interested in hearing them. Some even said their families had lost all interest in listening to stories (Bar-Itzhak and Shenhar 1993).

Haviva Dayan was one of the most gifted narrators I encountered. Thanks to this gift, as well as her unique personality, her family continued to display interest in her stories, and she still told many of them. Nevertheless, and even though she still took an active part in the housework,[3] she was haunted by the fear that her status would change. Sometimes she articulated her apprehension explicitly, but more often her fears were expressed in the connections she drew between the incidents of daily life and the stories, by means of sayings and parables that stimulated her family's curiosity so that they pressed her to explain her meaning and tell the story she had been alluding to.

One of Haviva's frequent refrains was "old women are good and they say sweet things." At one of our meetings I asked her to explain what this meant. She referred me to her granddaughter Yaffa, who was sitting with us, saying that she could tell me. The granddaughter, a woman in her thirties, said that Haviva Dayan had a story about the expression that she frequently told the family in recent years. We both urged her to tell it to us. She agreed happily and began to tell the story of Mother Alaguz (IFA 16434).

The Tales of Mother Alaguz

The day Mother Alaguz was born, a penny appeared in her hand.[4] *A penny of those days. She clutched it in her hand, like that, when she came out of her mother's belly. Alongside the penny there was a note saying that the penny would support her for life.*

Days went by, and days came, on and on. Mother Alaguz grew up and got married. Mother Alaguz got old. Mother Alaguz became an old woman. Whenever she offered her penny to somebody and said: "Give me vegetables for this penny," they would say: "Go, mother Alaguz! Take that penny of yours, what is a penny worth? Go, take your penny," and they would give her vegetables.

She would go to the butcher and say to him: "Give me meat for this penny," and he would say to her: "Mother Alaguz, this penny is worthless. Take the meat and go away, and take your penny."

Over and over again, over and over again. All those she went to told her the same thing.

One day she went out and bought a bundle of fish. As she was carrying the fish, there arose a storm, a storm and rain. She wrapped her head in a sheet. When she tried to raise her eyes she found herself at the entrance to the king's house, and around it guards are standing.

She said: "Now what is this? Where did this storm take me?"

They said to her: "This is the king's house."

She said to them: "What is this?"

The guard who was there said to her: "Oh, Mother Alaguz, why did you come now, in this storm, in these winds?"

She said to him: "Consult with the king on my behalf, and if he allows me to come in, I will get through the night and be fine, and if he does not allow me to come in, I will sit down here and I will die."

He went and told all this to the king.

The king said to him: "Go and bring this Mother Alaguz. . . . Old women are good, and they say sweet things. Go and bring her to amuse us a little."

Good, she entered. She kissed his hand, and she kissed his head. She sat down.

"Mother Alaguz, would you like something to eat, would you like something to drink?"

She said to him: "I will eat, and I will drink."

They brought her the food; they brought her the drink. When she came in, she found the king's wife standing. The king's wife snatched the bundle of fishes she was holding in her hand and swallowed them. His wife was a demon. She swallowed the fish, with the bones and with the innards.

Mother Alaguz said: "Woe! Now eat me for dessert! I will go to the king."

She went to the king. The king's wife came, poured them tea, brought them supper; they ate and drank.

The king said to her: "Tell me a story."

She said to him: "Till you finish your supper I will tell you the story, and dance and sing to you."

When the king had finished his supper, his wife brought him a cup with a sleeping draught. He drank it. When Mother Alaguz saw that he was asleep she too wrapped herself in her sheet and left a small chink in her sheet. Through the chink she watched the king's wife, to see what she was doing. The king's wife left. She left, and Mother Alaguz rose and followed her, slowly, slowly, slowly, to the back of the house. The she-demon called her mother: "Oh mother! Oh mother!"

She answered her: "Yes."

She said to her: "Let me, Mother, eat supper, or I will eat you and the king!"

"Go, you madwoman. You will eat me and the king for supper?!"

She said to her: "Go and get me some supper, or else I will sup on you and the king!"

She said to her: "Go, here are two mules. Their owner has brought them a short time ago. Go see them in the stable and eat them for supper, and I will pay the owner tomorrow morning."

She went there, and Mother Alaguz watches her all the time.

She went there and entered this stable. She stretched out her hand and tore the innards out of the belly of one of the animals, stretched out her hand again and tore out the innards of the other animal, and sat down. She eats and tears [the innards] to pieces again, and again, and again, and again, and again. She started eating their flesh, and they bray.

And Mother Alaguz watches all this—until she finished.

When she licked the bones, Mother Alaguz left, wrapped herself up, and fell asleep.

The woman—when she was finished she went to the shower, washed, changed her clothes, and went to sleep beside the king.

Good, dawn broke. The she-demon brought the king a cupful of drink to counteract the effect of the sleeping draught.

She said to him: "My lord, drink this cup of cold water so you recover and get up."

The king drank, got up, and wandered about in his house. The woman went and brought tea, and brought milk, and brought all she brought. They ate and drank, and the king left.

At night, the king said to Mother Alaguz again: "Oh Mother Alaguz, you did not tell us anything yesterday."

She said to him: "Oh my Lord, what shall I tell you? You had supper, and you fell asleep. Perhaps you want me to tell the walls something? Stay awake, and I will tell you stories, and sing and dance for you."

And she did not want to tell him about all she had seen in connection with his wife.

Again the she-demon brought them supper. They finished their supper, and she gave him the same cup again. He drank it and fell asleep. When

Mother Alaguz saw him like that, she covered herself with her little sheet and left the same chink open to peep through and watch.

The she-demon said: "They are all asleep." She went, opened the house and stepped outside. And Mother Alaguz followed her. She walks, and she follows her. She came to her mother: "Oh mother! Oh mother!"

She said to her: "Yes."

She said to her: "Give me some supper, or I will eat you and the king."

"Go, you madwoman, oh you madwoman! Oh you crazy woman. People pay millions to see the king, and you want to eat him for supper?"

She said to her: "If that is so, give me something for supper because I am hungry. Tonight I am hungry."

She said to her: "Go, there is a pair of camels. Their owner brought them here. Eat them for supper, and tomorrow I will pay for them."

She entered the stable and found those two camels. She stretched out her hand and tore out their innards and ate them. Mother Alaguz stood and watched. When she had finished the innards she started tearing off their flesh, and they brayed with pain. And so on, until she finished eating. When she was licking the bones, Mother Alaguz returned and fell asleep. The she-demon returned, went to the shower, washed, put on a new dress, and went to sleep beside the king.

The next morning, she brought him the cupful of drink again in order to wake him. He woke, recovered, and walked about and observed. The woman went downstairs to get the milk, the coffee, everything. Mother Alaguz said: "Oh my Lord."

He said to her: "Yes."

She said to him: "You are married to a she-demon."

"What did you say, oh Mother Alaguz?!"

She said to him: "You are married to a she-demon. If she is not a she-demon, kill me."

He said to her: "And how do you know that?"

She said to him: "Now I will not tell you anything. I will stay with you until nightfall, and then you can go with me and see everything. But there is one thing you must do."

He said to her: "What is that?"

She said to him: "When you finish your supper and she serves you a cup of tea, put a towel on your lap, and when she hands you the cup of tea, pour it onto the towel and keep quiet. Even if she shakes you, do not move."

Good. The woman went and brought them coffee, brought them tea; they drank; they ate; they drank.

The she-demon said to Mother Alaguz: "Mother Alaguz, come, come down, I want to tidy up the house."

The king went to his government house. They cooked dinner and ate.

The she-demon cooked supper and carried it to the king. He ate. Again, she brought him the same cup. He put the towel on his lap, emptied the contents of the cup into the towel, and kept quiet. The she-devil returned, shook him, and he did not move. Mother Alaguz peeped through the chink in the sheet, pretended she was asleep, and said neither yes nor no.

The she-demon left again. She went down, down, down, down, until she got there.

"Oh my mother! Oh my mother!"

She said to her: "Yes."

She said to her: "Get me some supper, or else I will sup on you and the king."

"Go, oh you madwoman. Sup on the king?! People pay millions to see him, and you want to eat him!?"

She said to her: "Tonight I am hungry, get me something to eat."

She said to her: "Go, there are two donkeys. Their owner brought them here and put them in the stable. Eat them, and tomorrow I will pay the owner."

She went where these donkeys were. And the king stands there and watches. He and Mother Alaguz. When the she-demon left, Mother Alaguz rose and said to him: "My lord."

He said to her: "Yes."

She said to him: "Rise, come with me to see your wife."

He went with her. He stood there, looked, and trembled all over.

He said to her: "Oh Mother Alaguz, this [creature] will not let go until she finishes me. And now, what am I to do?"

She said to him: "What you are going to do? Tomorrow at first light take a hundred guards with you. They must dig a well for you, and they must not throw away the earth, but leave it beside the well. And put up a tent over the well, and slaughter a sheep and call people, and call musicians and call singers. When they come, call your wife and tell her: 'Put on your gold [ornaments], and put on your dress and go and watch the musicians and the games.' And you cover the well with a carpet and place a small chair on it. When she comes, tell her: 'Come and have a look at the tent, you have never seen it before.' When she comes and sits down, she will fall into the well, and that is what is going to save you. If that does not save you, nothing will save you."

He went, the way it has been told, and did so. He sent the guards and slaughtered the sheep. They got the pots ready and prepared couscous.[5] *They dug the well, put the carpet across the well, and put up the tent.*

So the people ate and drank, and they left. Only the king and his wives stayed behind, and Mother Alaguz and the servant girls.

When his wife was leaving, the king said to her: "Come and have a look at this tent, you have never seen such [a tent] before." She entered.

He said to her: "Sit on this small chair."

She sat on the chair and fell into the pit.

The she-demon cried: "Oh king, this is treachery! Oh king, this is treachery!"

And he did not answer her.

The guards came. They shoveled the earth back into the pit, more, and more, until the pit was filled.

They went home. Mother Alaguz said: "Oh my lord, I wish to leave."

He said to her: "Oh Mother Alaguz, sleep and stay until the next day, and I will give you a saddle-bag of flour, a saddle-bag of sugar, I will give you oil, I will give you salted butter, I will give you . . ."

She said to him: "I will not take anything. I will not take anything from you except my little penny. I brought it here, in my hand, and I dropped it. Return it to me."

The king said to her: "Oh Mother Alaguz, sleep over, and I will command [the servants] to cut sheets for you, and I will give you a warm dress, I will give you . . . I will give you . . ."

She said to him: "I have everything."

So he kissed her hand and her head and said to her: "This is in return for saving me and for what you have done for me."

He gave her her little penny, and she went away, away, away, away.

Again there came rain and stormy winds, stormy winds. She put her kerchief on her head, and she did not know where she was going.

On, and on, and on, till nightfall. Again she found herself at the entrance to the house of a king. The guards rose and said to her: "Mother Alaguz, what made you come here at such a time?"

She said to them: "The stormy winds brought me here, the wind brought me, and now go and speak to the king and tell him about me."

They said to the king: "One Mother Alaguz does not know where to spend the night. She said: 'If he lets me stay here, I will stay, and if he does not, I will lie down till I die.'"

The king said to them: "Go and bring her in. Old women say sweet things. Tell the king's sick daughter, and maybe, with God's help, the king's daughter will answer."

She entered, as has been told. She kissed the hand and the head of his wife, who was sitting next to him.

She said to them: "What happened to you? Why are you sitting there, stunned and sad, why do you not laugh and play?"

He said to her: "Oh Mother Alaguz! I was barren and did not beget children until I begot one daughter. And she does not talk and does not allow anyone to enter her room. They bring her food and close the door." She said to him: "I will go to her. I will go and dance for her, and I will go and sing for her, and I will do everything to make her talk."

Good. They took her to her room. When she entered, she was sitting on a chair. When she saw Mother Alaguz, she threw herself on the bed, covered herself, and pretended she was asleep.

"Oh the king's daughter, good evening, oh the king's daughter."

But the king's daughter does not answer.

They brought her some tea.

"The king's daughter! Have a cup of tea, maybe you have not had anything to drink today."

No answer.

They brought them supper. Mother Alaguz ate.

"The king's daughter, rise and have supper, maybe you have not had anything to eat today. The king's daughter, the king's daughter." But there was no answer.

So what did Mother Alaguz do? She looked around and noticed that the king's daughter was staring at a wardrobe.

Mother Alaguz said to herself: "Good, there is something in that wardrobe. I will not go to sleep tonight."

She wrapped herself up in her scarf and left a chink open through which she watches this daughter of a king. A tiny, tiny chink. It was night. Nobody goes upstairs, and nobody goes downstairs. The king's daughter took the key that was on top of the wardrobe, opened the wardrobe, and took out a boy who was so beautiful that he would say to the sun: "You shine, or else I will shine. The God that created you created me."

He fell on her, kisses and embraces her, kisses and embraces, and she, too, kissed and embraced him. He lifted her on his shoulders, and they danced, ate, and drank. They played, they danced, they sang; there was nothing they did not do.

When the crier started calling,[6] *he said to her: "That's enough."*

She put him into the wardrobe. She locked him up and put the small key on top of the wardrobe and pretended she was asleep.

Then Mother Alaguz said to herself: "Now I too will go to sleep."

In the morning, they brought them some tea.

"The king's daughter, good morning, maybe you stayed awake at night, and maybe you are hungry . . ."

No answer.

Mother Alaguz drank her tea and went downstairs.

The king said to her: "Mother Alaguz, did she speak to you? Was there anything she talked about? Did she utter a word?"

She said to him: "Sir, the king's daughter talked to the one she loves, and those she does not love she does not talk to."

The king's wife rose. She said to her: "Mother Alaguz, you should be ashamed to say these things! Her door is locked. Nobody can get to her. Nobody goes to her, and nobody comes."

She said to them: "Shut up! I am the one who knows everything. And now, may God leave you in peace."

"Oh Mother Alaguz, sit down. Here is some money, take it. Here is some tea, take it. Here is some salted butter, take it."

She said to them: "I will not take anything. I will take nothing. The penny I dropped, give it to me."

They gave her her penny. She left. She walked, and she walked, and she walked. It grew dark again. Rain came. Wind came, a storm came, and it was night. She keeps on walking, and nothing matters to her except walking. Again she arrives at the door of the king's house. The guards rose and said to her: "Oh Mother Alaguz! Is this the time for a human being to arrive? The sky is black, and there are storms."

She said to them: "My feet carried me here, and I just bow my head and walk. And now speak to the king and tell him about me. If he says 'Let her come!' you send for me, and if he does not say 'Let her come,' I will sleep here, and if I die, may God be with me and grant me peace."

They spoke to the king and told him about her. The king said to them: "Go and send her in!"

When they sent her in they said to her: "Mother Alaguz, be careful, perhaps the king will see you and kill you."

She said to them: "Why?"

They said to her: "The king and all the town are in mourning, do you not see that the whole town is black and in mourning, and the king is in mourning, and his wives are in mourning, his servant girls are in mourning, and you are wearing your white, clean scarf, be careful, lest they put you in jail."

She said to them: "Just let me in, and the rest is none of your business."

Good, she came before the king, she kissed his hand, she kissed his head.

"May God grant you safety, why do you mourn? The king never mourns. Why? Tell me why, and perhaps with God's help salvation will come through me and we'll see what is to be done."

The king said to her: "What can I tell you? Let it be, Mother Alaguz, and keep silent."

She said to him: "Just tell me. I will not leave before you tell me what happened to you. Why does the whole town mourn, and why do you mourn?"

He said to her: "Oh Mother Alaguz, I married a hundred women but one, and for twelve years I did not beget a child. And this woman is the hundredth. There is nothing I did not do: I visited the tombs of the saints, and I took medicine, and this woman bore me a child. When he was fourteen years old, he went hunting with the guards. He hunted the first day, he hunted the second day, and on the third day he did not return with them. And now four years have gone by since he left, and he must be eighteen. I lost three or four thousand men when I had the mountains, hills, and val-

leys searched. I was hoping they might find him, find the bones of the horse. Nothing. The search parties do not return, wolves prey on them. And now that I have not found him for four years, the whole town mourns him."

She said to him: "My lord, I will say two words."

He said to her: "What, oh Mother Alaguz?"

She said to him: "Rise, send a town crier. All the houses are to be painted, one house green and the next white, and the whole town will be whitewashed. And you have your house whitewashed, and take off your mourning clothes, you and your wife and the servant girls, wash and put on clean clothes and clean the streets. And all will be well."

"Oh Mother Alaguz, what is the meaning of what you are saying?"

She said to him: "I will tell you the most important thing later. You just do as I told you, and you will see."

He went and sent the town crier, as I said before. He decreed: "Listen! Everybody must paint his house either green or white."

The world was bright and shining. All the houses were whitewashed. They woke, they drank tea. The king drank tea, and they gave Mother Alaguz tea.

She said to him: "Of all your helpers, who do you love best? Do you love the Kadi best, or the vizier, or the deputy vizier? Take what is most dear to you and be on your way."

The king rode on one side, the vizier on the other, and Mother Alaguz was in the middle. Forward, forward, forward. And they asked about the town about which, when leaving it, Mother Alaguz asked: "What is the name of the town where the king's daughter won't talk?"

They said to her: "The name is Halama, the city of Halama."

They looked for the city of Halama, on and on and on, until they found it. When they wanted to enter the town, she said to him, to the king: "I will tell you two words."

He said to her: "Which words, oh Mother Alaguz?"

She said to him: "Are you and the king of Halama close friends?"

He said: "Yes."

"In what way are you close?"

"We used to ride on horseback, to wander about to see kings, to throw parties and to talk to them."

She said to him: "Good, go and ask them: 'Where is the king of Halama?' till they show him to you. When you go to see him, kiss him. When he says to you: 'Why did you come, oh king? Welcome! For what reason did you come?' tell him: 'I want to have a look at your house and build one like it. I wanted to send emissaries, but I feared they would not understand the plan of the house, and therefore I have come by myself.' And when he takes you and wants to open the last room for you, say to him: 'No, open the room in the middle for me.' When he opens it, start walking around and observing from a small opening above. Take him aside and say: 'This door, where does it lead?' Do not mention the word "wardrobe." Just open the wardrobe, and bring the youth that is in there."

He said to her: "Oh Mother Alaguz, and if I do not find the key?"

She said to him: "The key is there, just lift your eyes."

He went, as has been narrated, and came to the king, the king of Halama. "My lord, what is it you wish? Why did you yourself come here?"

He said to him: "My friend, I was told about your house and about the decorations, and I wanted to build a house like that, and I was afraid to send a messenger, and that is why I myself came."

He said to him: "Welcome, welcome, welcome, come in. Drink tea."

He said to him: "I won't drink before I have not seen the house."

He went, as has been narrated, showed him the house. He wanted to open the last room. He said to him: "No! Open the room in the middle. People only want to see the middle part, but they do not take any notice of [the rooms] at the end."

He opened the room in the middle for him. He and the vizier entered the room. They walked about, he lifted his eyes and lo and behold! he sees the small key. He picked it up. He said: "This door—where does it lead?"

He opened the door, and the youth jumped on him. He lifted him on his shoulders and danced with him, danced, danced. But the king of Halama fell down; he fainted.

He said to him: "King of Halama!"

He said to him: "Yes."

He said to him: "Your daughter is a whore. You say: 'She is sick, she won't talk and does not let anyone in!' I have been sending out search parties for four years, and they do not return. Wolves ate them; demons tore them to pieces. The whole world looks for my son, on the hills and in the valleys, and she—hid him in the wardrobe?! If she had been my daughter, I would have cut her up into four pieces, and would have her thrown into the sea."

The unhappy king was shame-faced; the poor man had no answer. He said to him: "Oh almighty God, may God not burn the liver.[8] *This is the only daughter we have."*

He said to him: "I married a hundred women but one, until finally [the hundredth wife] bore me this son. I had to look for him; it took me four years to find him. I will proclaim that people may no longer be tried by you, and your government will no longer be allowed to rule. Get rid of this daughter; she is corrupt."

Good. He took his son and left.

"My lord, I will give you my daughter, even if she is going to be a servant. She got used to your son . . ."

He said to him: "Be quiet so I don't cut off your head with this sword."

He took the youth and put him on the horse's back, he took Mother Alaguz and danced with her all the way, until she said: "That's enough."

When they came to town he sent the proclamation to let the people know that the king's son had been found. Everybody came running to see the king's son. The horses run about, people play games, the orchestra plays, the songs, the flags, and the women yell.

Good, at last the people dispersed, they left.

The king said: "Oh my son."

He said to him: "Yes."

He said to him: "Don't you leave the house. You will learn how to rule. The day will come, and I will die, and the money and the property will be left, and there won't be anyone to inherit it. You must learn to rule in my stead.

Good, that is how it was. The son followed him everywhere. On, and on, and on. One month passed, two months. One night as they were sitting [in the room], the king of Halama came. He brought two oxen, put his daughter and his wife on a mule, and brought two camels laden with salted butter, honey, oil, all kinds of good things, and thus he came.

The guard asked: "What is it you want?"

He said to him: "Call the king."

The guard went to the king, and said to him: "My lord, my lord, put your hand on your head and say: 'I forgive.'"

He said to him: "God will forgive you if you tell the truth."

He said to him: "There is a man with a woman and a girl on a mule, and he rides a mule and there are two oxen with him."

The king said to his wife: "That is the king of Halama. He has brought his daughter in order to entreat me to marry my son to her." He left [the room], as has been narrated, and found the king of Halama.

The king of Halama fell upon him and kissed his head.

"Oh my lord! Hide what God has hidden. Oh my lord! Hide what The Creator has hidden. We are both kings. This is the only daughter I have. And we did not want to impose our will on her. And she is used to your son and loves him. And now let her be a servant in your kitchen, provided only that he weds her, so people say: 'She married a king.' If you want her, she will stay with you, and if you don't want her, I will come and take her away. Provided that she is considered as a person that is married to a king."

Good, as has been narrated they had a big wedding, and there is no

Haviva Dayan narrating the Mother Alaguz tales (Courtesy of Israel Folktale Archives)

Haviva Dayan with young listeners (Courtesy of Israel Folktale Archives)

one greater than God. She stayed there and lived with him. He built her a house. And the king's son also married the minister's daughter and built a house for her. Good, so they live and eat and drink. And the tale flows with the rivers. And our friends are generous givers.

This story has many of the key features of Moroccan Jewish folktales told by women. Especially typical is the concluding formula "And the tale flows with the rivers. And our friends are generous givers." The first half of the formula marks the transition from the world of the story to that of real life and daily discourse, while the second half thanks the listeners and asks them to reward the narrator for her story. Also typical of the stories of Moroccan Jewish women are the mention of God every time the word "great" is used and the addition of the phrase "and there is no one greater than God."

We are dealing with a conglomerate of several narrative types—a frame tale about the wanderings of Mother Alaguz, in which are embedded accounts of three incidents that occur in places where Mother Alaguz interrupts her travels. The first inner story, about the king and his demon wife, could stand on its own. The other two, about the silent princess and about the lost prince, are linked; solving the mystery of one makes it possible to solve the other as well.

Thus the structure of the story is as follows:

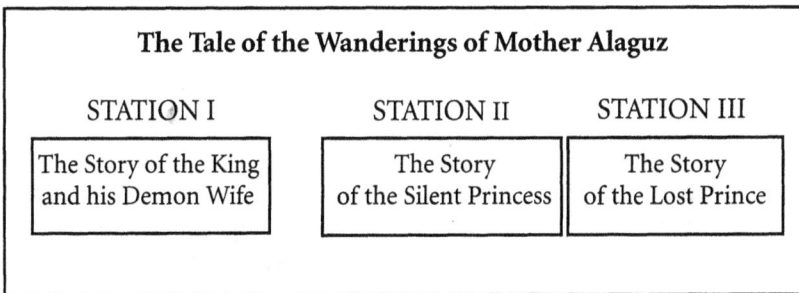

The Tale of the Wanderings of Mother Alaguz		
STATION I	STATION II	STATION III
The Story of the King and his Demon Wife	The Story of the Silent Princess	The Story of the Lost Prince

Even though most of the plot takes place when the heroine, Mother Alaguz, is an old woman, the frame tale actually begins with her birth, with the unusual circumstance that explains what is special about her. Their extraordinary birth is a key item in the heroes of myth and legend and of culture heroes in general, as many have noted (Raglan 1956; Rank 1959; Dundes 1978, 223–62).

In the story of Mother Alaguz, unlike myths or sacred legends, the circumstances are rather droll. The heroine is born clutching a small coin (Motif N121.1), which is supposed to support her as long as she lives. The humoristic element the penny introduces to the story is expressed in several ways. First there is the inversion: an object of paltry value—a farthing—supports her throughout her life. Second is the explanation of how this comes about: merchants prefer to give her their wares for free rather than take the penny from her. Finally we have the disproportion when kings offer the heroine valuable gifts that she declines, preferring to hold fast to her penny.

But the penny also serves as a means to explain her character and personality: an individual who can make do with a farthing and asks for no reward from those she benefits is independent and self-sufficient. The narrator creates a commonsensical, independent, and self-confident woman who is afraid of no one and stands up to courtiers and kings, negotiating with them and helping them without demeaning herself. There is an inversion of roles here; instead of the mighty kings assisting a helpless old woman, she is the one who solves their problems, which they are unable to understand. The inversion is highlighted at the end of the first embedded tale, when the king kisses Mother Alaguz's hand and head—an obeisance normally performed by his subjects (including the heroine at their first meeting) to him. It is hard to miss that the narrator, Haviva Dayan ("Mother Haviva" as she was called by her family), is creating a heroine in her own likeness—Mother Alaguz.

In international folk literature, the stories most similar to the tales of Mother Alaguz belong to Aarne and Thompson type 874 (AT 874), "the proud king is won" (1961). The plot framework of these stories resembles the stories of Mother Alaguz: a girl is asked to perform difficult tasks, rises to the challenge, and goes on a journey, solving problems wherever she comes. Where these stories differ from the Mother Alaguz story is in the type of heroine, why she begins her journey, and the conclusion. In AT 874 stories the heroine is a young girl in love with a proud prince who will marry her only if she performs the tasks. After she succeeds in them she does marry the prince. The variants noted by Aarne and Thompson come from the Mediterranean cultural basin— Sicily, Yugoslavia, and Turkey. Wolfram Eberhard and Pertev Boratav list eighteen variants of the type (1953, 188). The Israel Folktale Archives contain six Jewish versions of this type, from Greece, Morocco, Libya, Syria, Eretz Israel Sephardi, and Turkey.[9] Why did the narrator change the young heroine into an old woman?

Through Mother Alaguz the narrator created a character like herself, an independent old woman blessed with common sense and initiative, who knows how to get by in every situation. She is not afraid of natural disasters or of palace guards, of mighty rulers or supernatural beings. These traits help her solve the problems of others. We should note that all the problems involve relations between spouses and between parents and children, where an old woman's experience is a sterling asset. The powerful and mighty need her assistance and advice, while she asks for nothing in return. Her reward is the very act of solving problems and the esteem this wins her. Listeners realize the value of old women, about whom kings declare "they are good and say sweet things."

When Haviva Dayan told the stories of Mother Alaguz, she was telling about herself. Weaving a fascinating, frightening, and entertaining story that drew on the folk literature of her native country, she embedded in it her hopes and aspirations—the hopes of an elderly Jewish woman who has experienced the vicissitudes of fate and cultural change and seeks an honored place in the Israeli society that is now her home, for herself and those like her.

A Moroccan Cinderella in an Israeli Context

According to Richard Bauman, a contextual and ethnographic approach to narrative enables discovery of "the individual, social, and cultural factors that give it shape and meaning in the conduct of social life" (1986, 2). Following Bauman's suggestions, I would like to preface detailed analysis of one particular storytelling event with a brief description of its social and cultural context.

In this storytelling event an elderly woman told a story familiar to many Moroccan Jewish women. The situation in which she told it is a direct consequence of the far-reaching changes in the values and norms of Moroccan immigrants, in everything associated with family life that took place in Israel. As we shall see, the narrator used a well-known and beloved folktale to convey a message in a severe conflict situation that had erupted in her family.

The Smeda Rmeda narrative that follows was narrated by storyteller Freha Hafutah, a ninety-year-old blind woman who comes from the Atlas Mountains in Morocco. She came to Israel with her four children in 1955. Freha has had no formal education and claims that her wisdom comes from the folk narratives she heard when she was young in Mo-

Freha Hafutah
(Courtesy of Israel
Folktale Archives)

rocco. Her narrative was recorded on our first meeting when I came to her house with a group of researchers and students (all women).

When we entered Freha's home, she was resting on a bed in the hall-way. Her daughter had gone to the market, but returned as we were recording the first narrative and sat down to join the listeners. In the next room, which served as the living room, a man was lying on a sofa. He introduced himself as Avraham, and when we asked Freha to nar-rate, we asked him if he, too, knew some narratives. He replied, "I don't listen to the nonsense of old people" and left the room. We then sat in a circle around Freha, who began to speak. Her narrative was humor-ous and made everybody laugh. During the course of the storytelling, Avraham returned and started walking among the listeners, and as the narrative drew to a close he responded together with us. When it was over, he served us coffee. It was to this audience of researchers, students, and family members that the narrator addressed herself when she told the Smeda Rmeda narrative.

Smeda Rmeda[10]

Vocal Characterizer		*Kinesic Features*
piano larghetto	Let me tell you, God was every-where, but he was in our hands and in the listeners' hands. Our house is silk and cotton, but the house of the Moslems will be ruined and all the Moslems will be destroyed in a single day.	holds the hand of the nearest listener
accelerando	There was, let me tell you, a certain woman. She had just one son and one daughter—that was all she had in the whole world. The girl used to go out with her girl friends every day: she went to school with them, combed her hair with them, and played and laughed with them.	
a tempo	One of God's fine days the neighbor—the mother of the girls—said to her:	
harsh	"Listen, why are you always hanging around my daughters? Your mother does not pay any at-tention to you, and does not love you, and does nothing for you.	
seductive	You must kill her."	
childish	She said to her: "How do you want me to kill my mother? What for?"	
harsh	She said to her: "What should you do? Get a snake and put it in the butter jar."	moves hand in a circle around the audience
conversational	(Let's get on with the story, dear friends.)[11]	

childish	So the girl said to her: "How am I to kill my mother?"
harsh	She said to her: "Get the snake and put it in the butter jar and pretend you are sick and go to sleep, and tell her: 'Mother, cook a little Barkuksh for me.'[12]
	"And when she says: 'Rise, oh her brother, go and get the butter,' tell her: 'His hands are not clean.'
	"'Rise, oh her father, go.'
	"Tell her: 'His hands are hairy.'
	"'Rise, oh the servant, go.'
	"Tell her: 'Her hands are black. Mother, you go.'
	"And when she goes and gets the butter, she dies. And then your father will come and ask me to be his wife, and you will be the dearest person in the whole world to me."
	Good. This is what the poor girl did.
childish	She went to her mother and told her: "I am not going to school today."
obliging	"Why, my daughter?"
	"I am sick, mother, sick."
	She said to her: "My daughter, what can I do for you?"
	She said to her: "I want to sleep."
	She slept. And the poor mother made her bed lovingly and put her to bed.
devotedly	"I am your Kappara,"[13] she said. "What can I do to help you?"
	She said to her: "Just cook a little Barkuksh for me."

secretive	And she had already put the viper into the opening of the butter jar—	
conversational	(May God spare us such misfortune.)	turns to the listeners
	The daughter was asleep and the mother wanted to cook some Barkuksh for her.	
	"Rise, oh her brother. Go and get the butter."	
	She said to him: "Your hands are dirty."	
	"Rise, oh the servant, and go."	
	"Her hands are black."	
	"Rise, oh her father, and go."	
commanding	"No, father's hands are hairy. Mother, you go. Wash your hands."	
emphatic	Good. She got up from her chair, washed her hands, the poor woman—	
conversational	(May you not see misfortune.)	turns to the listeners
	The moment she stepped into that cursed cellar to get the butter the viper attacked her. The mother died.	
conversational	(May YOU not see misfortune and may you not see evil.) She died, the poor woman.	turns to the listeners
adagio	Good, seven days went by, eight days, time went by.	moves her hand in a circle
	(Now don't you say anything!)[14]	turns to the listeners
accelerando	One day the girl rose and went out with the daughters of the neighbor as usual. She goes out with them, washes, takes a shower, and gets dressed.	

harsh	She said to her: "Now that your father is alone with you and your brother, go and tell him, tell your father to marry me, and you	
tempting	will be the dearest person in the world to me."	
pleading	Good, she went to her father, and said to him:	
	"Father, the kind of life we are leading is not good. Will you remain without a wife? There is our neighbor whom we love and who is a close friend. Marry her, and she will take care of us."	
	He said to her: "Oh my daughter, there is no time for a wedding."	gesture of rejection
	She implored him, the poor girl, and he married her. He married the neighbor.	
	Now don't you say anything! What did her seven daughters do? They stood above the father's beard, her father, and relieved themselves.	
apologetic	(If you will excuse me.)	turns to the listeners
	They soiled his beard and his clothes.	
	The poor man rose: "Oh my God, who did this to me?"	
forceful and harsh	She said to him: "I weep for you and your daughter."	waves hand from inside outside
apologetic	(Excuse me.)	turns to the listeners
	"By God, my daughter would never do such a thing, neither she nor her brother. Don't you dare to say a thing like that."	

harsh   She said to him: "What can we   shakes head
                         do to her? Let's lock her up in the
                         baking room for the night, and
                         you will see what she does."

                         They grabbed her and locked her
                         up there for the night. The next
                         morning, the father woke up in
                         the same state as before, and they
                         did this to him day after day.

secretive   The girls would climb up to the
                         opening in the roof, above the
                         baking room, and they would
                         do it.

                         The neighbors protested: "By
protesting   God, oh my daughter, do you
                         think there is something wrong
                         with the daughter of your
                         husband? She leaves the baking
                         room, relieves herself, and goes
                         back. And they lock her up in the
                         room, the poor girl."

                         (Don't you say anything, my dear   turns to the listeners
                         friends!)

                         Time passes, and the king's son
                         announces that he is looking for
                         a wife.

                         Nobody stayed indoors, not even
                         drummers, buglers, or people
                         who scour their faces with red-
                         hot loam.[15]

                         (Don't you say anything, my   turns to the listeners
                         dear!)

                         The father of the unlucky girl
                         who was locked in the room
                         where the oven was wanted to go
                         to Marrakesh.

                         The girls said to him: "Bring me
                         a kerchief."

                         And another girl said: "A pair of
                         slippers."

And another: "A dress."

He rose and said to his wife: "Oh my daughter, I will go to the orphan and ask her, too, what she wants."

harsh

"Sit down, sit down," she told him. "You just sit down. She is covered all over with soot and excrement, you have no reason to go and ask her."

waves hand from below upwards

decisive

He said to her: "No. I will go to her, poor girl that she is."

He went to the baking room; he said to her: "I am going to Marrakesh to do some shopping. The king's son is looking for a wife, and my wife's daughters have told me what they want me to buy for them. Now what do you want me to buy for you?"

piano

She said to him: "Father, just bring me seven nuts."

He said to her: "Very good, oh my daughter."

compassionate

Good, he went to Marrakesh, and he bought ever so many things, but he forgot all about the seven nuts, the poor fellow. On the way home he remembered and went back to Marrakesh. What did he buy?

He bought a sack full of nuts. But the sack had a hole, and as he was walking the nuts fell to the ground, until there were only seven nuts left.

apologetic	He returned; he brought her the nuts. He said to her: "Daughter, take these nuts. They are what God and your luck gave you. I brought you a sack, my daughter, and now—"	
	She said to him: "Father, give them to me. These seven nuts are enough to bring me luck—God will give me luck."	
	Good. She took the seven nuts and hid them.	
conversational	The king was getting married. The stepmother (may you be spared such calamities) gathered together all kinds of grain and kernels—barley, wheat, corn—everything, mixed them in one room, and climbed up to the attic.	turns to the listeners
harsh and highly pitched	She said to her: "If you don't sort these out and put each grain where it belongs, I'll cut the ground beneath your feet."	
	She sent the girl to that room. The girl cried—the moment she wiped one eye, the other eye started getting wet.	drying eyes
secretive	She cracked the first nut. The nut was empty.	
	She cracked the second nut. Samsam-Kamkam came out.[16] When the demon came out, her luck appeared.	spreads hands to show his size
	"Whatever you wish, my Lady— it will be done."	
melancholy	She said to him: "You see what a fix I am in, don't you?"	

Good, he worked, sorting out everything. This goes here, in this sack, and that goes there, in that sack, and again in that sack. He sewed up the sacks and the room was spotless. Then he left and disappeared.

The poor girl cracked the third nut. Someone appeared—his horse was green, his headgear was green, his dress was green, and his sword was green to match.

He said to her: "Everything my Lady wants done will be done."

She said to him: "What my Lady wants done will be done? She wants to be taken from here to the king's wedding feast."

He took her, he carried her and turned her into a charming girl.

| conversational | (May God grant you this without a story and without a tale. May He grant you luck and may your husbands live.)[17] | turns to the listeners |

He turned her into a beautiful girl, carried her on his shoulders to the wedding feast of the king's son.

| mezza voice | The girls are talking, and one of them says: "Mother, Mother, Mother, there is our sister. Here she comes." | |

| conversational | The mother said to her: "Be quiet. That is the king's daughter." That is what the stepmother (may you be spared such a calamity) says. "This," she says, "is a princess, that poor girl is locked up in a dark room. | turns to the listeners |

Good. The people laugh and eat and drink. They laid a regal table for the girl, and she sits down, eats, drinks in the king's house, the house of the wedding.

allegro
retardando

Good. The wedding feast is over and the people left, and only she stayed. She cracked the first nut, found it was rotten, the second was rotten, until she got to the last nut, the seventh. She cracked it, and someone on horseback appeared. The horse was red, the headdress was red to match.

"Whatever my Lady wants done   bends head
will be done!"

commanding

"She wants to be taken away now, and she wants to be put in the baking room where her father's wife put her."

And the room is swept clean and there is nothing in it.

On her way back she lost one shoe. No other girl had a shoe like that, and who should find it but the king's son who was look- ing for a wife.

forte

He said: "There is only one per- son whom this shoe will fit."

All the girls living in that country were brought to him—all of them. The shoe was too large for one girl, too small for another.

They rose and said: "We tried them all. There is only one girl left, she is hidden in a baking room.

He said to them: "Fetch her."

harsh	The mother said to him: "This ought not to be done, sir. She is covered with excrement and soot, and what is she to be fetched for?"
commanding	He said to them: "Get her, no matter what."
	They brought her before him. He put the beautiful shoe on her foot, and it was a perfect fit.
	He said to her: "You are the one I am going to marry."
sardonic	"Sir, she does not suit you."
commanding	Good, the servant girls carried her to the bath-house, gave her a dress that suited her, took her, bathed her, dressed her, and took her to the king's son.

He made a big wedding feast, and only God is great. (May God grant you and us such a feast.) — lifts hand, turns to the listeners

(Don't you say anything!) The cursed woman, the father's wife, envied the girl. What did she do? The girl became pregnant, she was in an advanced stage of pregnancy, the poor girl.

harsh	(Don't you say anything!) The father's wife rose and said to her daughters: "Rise, come, let us go and visit your sister and see what God has given her."
fortissimo	(Envy!)
	(Don't you say anything!) They went to see her, they checked them over and let them in.
irony	The people said: "Her father's wife and her daughters?"
	Good, the king's son let them in.

sardonic

These women sit and say: "Come and we'll take you for a walk and cheer you up."

They took her for a walk and when they came to a well they threw her into it. In this well there lived lions and demons. They threw her into the well, and she fell onto the back of a lioness.

What did the sisters do? What did the mother do? She took her daughter, the one who was blind in one eye, put make-up on her face, dressed her, and sent her to the king's son.

The king's son came and talked to her, but she would not answer.

He said to her: "What happened to your eye?"

She said to him: "What happened to my eye? My brother grabbed me and gouged it out."

He said to her: "And what do you want me to do to your brother?"

whispering,
hypocritically

She said to him: "What do I want you to do to him? Let's slaughter him, put him into a loaf of bread and send him to our home."

sighing

He said to her: "Alright, oh my daughter."

And the poor brother heard everything. He went to that well, weeping, the poor boy. He said to her:

singing

"My sister, oh my sister,

Oh daughter of our father and mother,

The ovens are heating up

And the knives are being sharpened."

The poor girl rose and replied:

singing
"My brother, oh my brother,

Oh son of our father and mother,

I am caught between the lion and
the lioness,

And the king's sleeve is in my
hands

And the daughters of the women
have betrayed me."

(When I tell this tale, my tears   turns to the listeners
flow. It is heartrending.)

emphatic
Good, the king's son passed by
and found the boy sitting next to
the well, weeping, pleading with
her, listening to her (tale of woe).

He said to him: "Say that again,
my child. Repeat what you were
saying. Say it again!" He sat there
and said to her:

singing
"My sister, oh my sister, Oh
daughter of my father and
mother, The knives have been
sharpened, And the ovens are
heating up."

And she rises and replies:

singing
"My brother, oh my brother,

Oh son of our father and mother,

I am caught between the lion and
the lioness

And the sleeve of the king's son is
in my hands

And the daughters of the woman
have set me a trap."

(Don't you say anything, my   turns to the listeners
dear!) He said to him:

"Nice."

He went to the magicians, to the greatest of them and said to him: "Oh master, a boy beside the well is beseeching someone and somebody answers him from in-side the well, and I do not know who it is."

And the one-eyed one, her mother left her behind, she is hiding in the palace and does not want to talk to him.

The chief magician said to him: "Go ahead and slaughter seven oxen, slaughter them and throw them down that well."

Good. They did so.

accelerando "Oh, who did us this favor? Who did us this favor? We'll return it."

The girl appeared, she got off the   lifts hands
lioness's back and is holding the child.

compassionate She had given birth inside the well, the poor girl, inside the well.

She climbed from the well, hold-ing her child, and the king's son grabbed her.

"Oh my daughter, who did this?"

She said to him: "Come, come, come and be silent. The knives
conversational that were sharpened for my brother (may I never see such a   turns to the listeners thing happen to my brothers) and the ovens that are heating up will be heated up for the one-eyed girl, and she will be sent to our house in a sack."

a tempo	Good. He took her, he took the poor girl of whom the women said: "Smeda Rmeda who destroyed her good fortune with her own hands."
accelerando	(Don't you say anything!) This is what they did: they brought the blind girl, policemen took her, slaughtered her and cut her up, and they lit the bread oven and the meat oven, they took the blind head and hid it and put chunks of flesh in layers between some bread, and put it on a lame she-ass's back, and told the she-ass: "Go. Come back the way you started out."
fortissimo	"Hurrah," the mother rejoiced. Her daughter sent her a present, her daughter sent her a present. She feels good.

She took the sack, and gave everybody some bread and a piece of meat.   *moves hand as if dividing food*

"Here you are. Take some."

eulogizing	(Don't you say anything, my dear friends.) 'Til she got to the head, and recognized her daughter's head. Then she wailed: "All those who have shared bread with me—come and shed tears with me."	
conversational	(May God give you luck, and may your children and your husbands live.)	*turns to the listeners*

The girl was lucky, and they made a big wedding feast, but only God is great.

maestoso	And the tale floats on the rivers.

And you, my friends, are cheerful
givers.

Seven apples appeared, you ate one and another woman ate one, and yet another ate one, and Avraham took what was left. Good, I left Avraham out. Perhaps he married her.	bends fingers of the nearest listener

From my knowledge of the Jewish Moroccan folktale, I was familiar with the concluding formula in which the storyteller hands out imaginary apples to the audience and expects gratitude in return. While transcribing the text, however, I came across the name Avraham identified as one of the apple recipients. I found the concluding sentence particularly difficult to connect to the preceding narrative: "Perhaps he married her." Since the name Avraham did not appear among the characters of the story, we concluded that he was the man who was listening to the story with us. We knew very little about him from our brief encounter when we first arrived at Freha's home and learned of his ambivalent attitude toward her. Freha's intended message for him at the end of the story was a complete puzzle to us.

My additional meetings with the storyteller were a result of my desire to record more of her narratives, as well as to attempt to decode the message concealed in the concluding formula. At these other meetings, I learned additional details that finally made the decoding of the storytelling event and Freha's intended message possible.

It turns out that Freha lives in her daughter's home. The daughter's husband had divorced her because she was barren, which is legal according to Halachic Law, after a period of ten childless years. The daughter currently lives with Avraham, although the couple is unmarried. This lifestyle, although acceptable in secular circles in Israel, is contrary to Jewish faith and in contrast to socially sanctified norms held by Moroccan Jews. The population of the small Israeli town in which the family lives was, at that time, a homogeneous one of Moroccan Jews, who greatly disapproved of this living arrangement.

Freha was caught in an unbearable vise. On the one hand, she disapproved of her daughter's actions, which were in total conflict with her own views and the social norms of her community. On the other hand, she was totally dependent on her daughter for her livelihood. It turned out that Freha had made her disapproval known to the couple, which strained her relationship with them. In fact, at the time of our visit and the recording, their communication had nearly reached a breaking point. Avraham's declaration that he was not interested in listening to old people's nonsense was a direct outcome of this situation.

It was under these circumstances that Freha directed her message to only a small part of her audience, namely, her daughter and Avraham. However, it was the performance situation that arose, in which visitors were present and a humorous story was narrated, that motivated Avraham and Freha's daughter to join the event and become part of Freha's audience. In this setting Freha's status as storyteller was dominant, superseding the more problematic position she usually held in the household, which had interfered with communicative processes in the everyday life of this family. Those who would not usually listen to her became part of Freha's audience, and the presence of nonfamily members enabled her to overcome her fear of negative response from the couple. This is a type of situation that Barbara Kirshenblatt-Gimblett has called "performance as social interaction" (1975, 106–30).

As we seek to determine how the Smeda Rmeda narrative functions in this specific storytelling situation, the question that arises is why Freha chose this narrative from her ample repertoire for the purpose of conveying her message. In order to answer this question, one must uncover the deeper structure and message of the narrative by analyzing its type and structure, which I have done below.

The Cinderella narrative is one of the most famous fairy tales in the Western world, and as such it has merited numerous typological studies. Among the classics are the works of Marian Roalfe Cox (1893), the Swedish folklorist Anna Birgitta Rooth (1951), and Antti Aarne and Stith Thompson (1961). In the introduction to his collection of articles on Cinderella, Alan Dundes compares the kinds of subtypes established by Cox, Rooth, and Aarne and Thompson (1982). The versions of Smeda Rmeda to be considered here may be classified as Cox's type A, Rooth's type B, and Aarne-Thompson types 510 and 510A.[18]

Aarne and Thompson list five basic narrative components of type 510:

I. The Persecuted Heroine
II. Magic Help
III. Meeting the Prince
IV Proof of Identity
V. Marriage with the Prince

In contrast to the international type, this narrative is characterized by an additional two episodes, which precede those identified by Aarne and Thompson. These may be defined as follows:

I. At the instigation of the woman who covets her father; the heroine kills her mother.

II. The heroine convinces her father that he should marry the woman who encouraged her to kill her mother.

In five of the seven versions from IFA, Smeda Rmeda kills her mother in accordance with the advice of her neighbor, a widow who wishes to marry her father. This murder is committed in conjunction with Smeda Rmeda's request for food. Sometimes the food is festive and nourishing, such as Barkuksh, a dish cooked with butter that has to be fetched from the cellar. In other versions the food requested is honey, which is also stored in a dark place. Sometimes the female storytellers tone down the murder: in one version the neighbor conceals a snake in the cellar; and to cause her mother's death, Smeda Rmeda merely has to ask her to go down and fetch the butter.[19]

In those versions where the mother is not killed directly by Smeda Rmeda, the marriage of the father and the stepmother also results from the daughter's pleas. Generally, the father tries to reject these pleas. He says: "The year of worrying will pass, and the year of festivity will come." But he finally gives in to his daughter's entreaties. This turn of events often prompts narrators' reference to the heroine as "Smeda Rmeda who destroys her luck with her own hands," a refrain that frequently recurs at critical points in the narrative.

These additional episodes, characteristic of Jewish Moroccan versions of the Cinderella tale, are not completely absent from the versions that were at the disposal of those who formulated the international tale type. Stith Thompson was familiar with the tale as it appears in Giambattiste Basile's *Il Pentamerone* of 1634, as Bruno Bettelheim has pointed out (1977, 242–44).[20] In Basile's version the heroine's mother dies and Zezolla's (the Cinderella-like character) father remarries. The heroine believes that her stepmother is scheming to destroy her and tells her nurse about it. The nurse suggests that Zezolla should kill her stepmother by dropping the lid of a box on her head, and then convince the father to marry the nurse. Zezolla complies with the wishes of her nurse. Once married to the heroine's father, the nurse brings her six daughters to live in the household and starts maltreating Zezolla.

Basile's version does not find full expression in the international tale type. This is probably because the occurrence in this version of the two episodes discussed above (matricide and the father's remarriage) appeared to be unique among known versions. However, the majority of Jewish versions of the Cinderella narrative recorded in Asia and Africa are characterized by the presence of these episodes,[21] as are those known to be told in a Moslem context.[22] It is to be assumed it is from the latter that this motif entered Jewish Moroccan storytelling.

For Bettelheim, Basile's version is significant because it clarifies the underlying Oedipal elements of the Cinderella narratives: the wish of a child to occupy the position of the parent of his or her own sex in the affections of the other parent, to be his beloved and even be a sex partner. Bettelheim uses this version to substantiate his thesis, as he certainly could have done with the Jewish Moroccan versions I have encountered. In fact, our versions contain additional references to Oedipal relations. In one, Smeda Rmeda's father is said to have "married [the neighbor], but on condition that his daughter should share his room because that was what she was used to." Another narrator says the neighbor "married him, but the daughter would not let go of her father. She would sleep with him in his bed."

The two episodes characteristic of the Jewish Moroccan versions also contribute to the particular depiction of the character of the heroine. In these versions, as in many European ones, the name of the heroine is associated with the ashes on which she must sit, symbol of her suffering: "Smeda Rmeda" suggests both fine flour, or semolina, and ashes.[23] Yet, while the international tale type begins with "The Persecuted Heroine," Smeda Rmeda is not portrayed as an innocent girl who suffers through no fault of her own. The two additional episodes make it clear that it is the heroine's unethical actions that lead to her suffering and humiliation, as is represented by her banishment to the cook-room or bakery. These locations constitute focal points in the domestic routine of the household and may symbolize the girl's wish to return to her murdered mother. Similarly, the ashes on which Smeda Rmeda sits may be suggestive of mourning, but they are equally suggestive of purification—a metaphor for the redemptive process the girl is undergoing (Bettelheim 1977, 253–55).

It is important that in addition to the other accusations leveled at the girl, our version charges the heroine with relieving herself in an inappropriate manner and place. In one of the versions, for instance, we learn the following:

One day—what did she do? The stepmother prepared an evening meal of chickpeas, to which she added handfuls of salt. She said to [the girl's father]: "Your daughter will eat that, and then she will drink." The father was not there. She handed the girl bowl after bowl of chickpeas—yallah, yallah, yallah. The next morning the girl soiled their bed [with excrement]. [The woman] said to him: "Now are you going to let your daughter spend the night with you?!" (IFA 4565)

This incident exemplifies the girl's lack of cleanliness, a theme that is typical of the Jewish Moroccan versions but that finds extreme expression in this one, where it involves the breaking of a taboo.

The second episode identified by Aarne and Thompson, "Magic Help," is also present in the Jewish Moroccan versions, although it takes on a slightly different character. None of the possibilities offered by the international type fits in with our narrative, although there is a certain resemblance between our versions and that of the Brothers Grimm (1960, 8–92). In the latter the heroine's stepsisters ask the father to bring them clothes and ornaments when he sets out on a journey, whereas in the Grimms' story the young Aschenputtel asks only for the branch of a walnut tree. This she plants on the grave of her mother. Later, the tree gives her magical gifts. In the Jewish Moroccan versions Smeda Rmeda desires walnuts, and it is similarly the father who brings home the object with supernatural powers. As in the Grimms' versions, the father gives the heroine a magical gift that ultimately enables her to leave his household. The walnuts themselves thus become associated with the end of the heroine's adolescence; in fact, nuts are generally associated with fertility in folk belief.

In the Jewish Moroccan narratives, the magical helpers who emerge from the walnuts are male giant-demons. This contrasts with many European versions in which female characters function as saviors, whether in the form of fairies, fairy doves, or animal reincarnation of the dead mother. In some of the Jewish Moroccan versions the giant-demons have names, and in others they merit detailed description. The character who appears most frequently is Samsam-Kamkam, or Samsam ben Kamkam, a giant "whose head is in the sky and whose feet are in the water."[24] His appearance foreshadows a change in the fortunes of the heroine: as one narrator puts it, "Samsam Kamkam appeared, and her luck returned." Sometimes the giant is characterized by being all green or all red, colors suggestive of fertility or, in the case of the latter, the first sexual act. The giant-demons address Smeda Rmeda using a fixed formula: "What Madame wants me to do will be done." This motif— marvelous giants who inhabit tiny objects and come to the assistance of their owners—is widely distributed in Eastern narratives. In the Smeda Rmeda story above, the giant-demons serve the heroine by sorting the seeds for her, bringing about her physical transformation by getting her beautiful clothes, transporting her to the palace, and when the ball is over, returning her home as requested.

The third episode of the international tale type, "Meeting the Prince," would better describe the Jewish Moroccan versions if titled "Going to the Ball": Smeda Rmeda does not meet the prince at all, and none of the three options offered by the international type materializes in our narrative. The Jewish Moroccan versions reflect the Eastern custom of the segregation of men and women: at the ball, Smeda Rmeda is said to eat and drink her fill and listen to songs, but she does not meet the prince. That the prince falls in love with her is a function of the shoe he finds.

In some versions a dramatic dimension is added to this discovery: the lost shoe falls into a well or a spring from which the king's horses drink. The horses refuse to drink because of the radiance emanating from the shoe, and this is how the prince discovers it. He falls in love with the owner of the shoe and announces that he will marry none but her. The motif of falling in love when finding a shoe is contained in the ancient Egyptian tale recounted by Strabo (1932, VIII, 93–94) in which an eagle grabs the sandal of the beautiful Rodophis as she is bathing, then flies to Memphis, where the king is administering justice, and drops it at his feet. The king so admires the exceptional beauty of the sandal that he instructs his servants to search all over Egypt for its owner so he can marry her. When the girl is found in the town of Naukratis, she is taken to Memphis and becomes the king's wife. Many researchers have pointed out that the shoe is an erotic object symbolizing sexual desire, inasmuch as it is a small receptacle that can be penetrated by a part of the body in a precise fit. Marian Cox notes that certain ethnic groups celebrated betrothal by putting on a shoe, while in central Europe people used to throw a shoe at newlyweds to ensure that their sex life would work out.[25] In Judaism the shoe is also linked with sex: the ritual of the *Halitzah* (the removal of the sandal of the wife's brother-in-law) is a case in point. Jacob Nacht argues that the shoe symbolizes Woman, and that this explains the *Halitzah* ritual. According to Nacht, the shoe is further connected to relations between the sexes in that it symbolizes authority (1959, 166–67).

"Recognition," the fourth narrative episode of the international tale type, occurs in our versions of the Smeda Rmeda story, too. As in Aarne and Thompson's variant IVa, Smeda Rmeda is recognized when she tries on the lost shoe. The shoe itself takes on several different shapes in the European versions: small and golden (Grimm), shiny and high-heeled (Basile), made of expensive satin (Scotland), a glass slipper (Perrault), and so forth. In the Jewish Moroccan versions the shoe is variously described as a slipper made of silver embroidered with gold thread, a beautiful green slipper, or, more generally, "a precious slipper, such as nobody has ever seen before." The shoe in the Jewish Moroccan narratives, as in most European versions, is not described as being particularly small.[26] The amputation of toes and heels performed by the stepsisters in the Grimms' tale is therefore a detail unnecessary to the Jewish Moroccan versions.

The fifth episode of the international type—"Marrying the Prince"—is equally present in our versions. With such an event at its conclusion, it is possible to regard the Cinderella narrative as a tale of maturation, moving from the mother's death, to the father's remarriage, to a period of adolescence, a time of degradation and humiliation, and finally, to the heroine's own marriage—the symbol of her maturity. But at this point we observe the difference between the Jewish Moroccan narratives and the versions at the disposal of Aarne and Thompson: the Smeda Rmeda narratives do not end with marriage. Instead, injury is inflicted upon the heroine, with one of the stepsisters disguised as Smeda Rmeda.[27]

In our narratives the stepmother sends one of her daughters, described as the ugliest of the lot and usually half blind, on a visit to Smeda Rmeda.[28] The stepsister pretends she wishes the heroine well. In three of our seven versions, the stepsister uses seven "blind" needles (needles without eyes) given to her by her mother to pierce Smeda's Rmeda's scalp while combing her hair. When the stepsister does this, Smeda Rmeda turns into a dove and flies away.[29] The stepsister then poses as the heroine, but the dove does not despair: she perches on a wall close to the prince's room and sings.

My father gave me things,
And my mother deceived me.
The king's son took me,
And he was kind to me,
And he gave me things.
Her daughter came and deceived me.

> Oh trees, be my witness.
> Weep over me!
> You stones, weep!
> Oh you son of the king,
> Weep for me at the gate of my palace.

When the dove finishes her song, the wall collapses. When this happens again, the king's son is mystified. He tars the wall and catches the dove.[30] As he strokes the dove, the prince notices the needles. He pulls them out, and Smeda Rmeda is restored to her true form.[31]

In the remaining four versions we are told at the beginning that Smeda Rmeda has a brother. Although this character disappears from the plot until after Smeda Rmeda's marriage, there is never any character in the folktale that does not perform some function, and indeed the brother performs his at this late stage. An Indian version of the Cinderella tale in which the heroine has a brother is cited by A. K. Ramanujan (1982, 259–85); but whereas the presence of a brother in the Indian narrative allows the plot to move in the direction of incest, this theme is absent from our versions. The narrative function of the brother in the Jewish Moroccan versions is different, as will be shown below.

In the Jewish Moroccan versions, the stepsister (who is blind in one eye) proposes to the pregnant heroine that they should go for a walk. When they come to the well from which lions and spirits drink or, alternately, to a room to which a taboo is attached, the stepsister pushes Smeda Rmeda into it and then poses as the heroine. When the prince expresses astonishment at the girl's visual handicap, she claims that her brother put out her eye and that as punishment he should be slaughtered and his flesh roasted. Meanwhile, Smeda Rmeda gives birth in the dark and perilous place. In these versions the truth of the situation emerges as the brother and sister express their woe. This dialogue is in rhyme in every version:

> My sister, oh my sister,
> Oh daughter of our father and mother,
> The ovens are heating up
> And the knives are being sharpened.
>
> My brother, oh my brother,
> Oh son of our father and mother,
> I am caught between the lion and the lioness,

And the king's sleeve is in my hands
And the daughters of the women have betrayed me.

Initially, the prince does not understand the meaning of this dialogue, but when he discovers the truth, he rescues his wife and child. Many elements of AT 403 IV, "The Substituted Bride," find expression here, such as the entrapment of the heroine and the reference to the birth of her child (AT 403 IVa), the impersonation of the true bride (IVc),[32] and the reference to the brother and the attempt to hurt him (IVd).

The final episode in the Jewish Moroccan versions involves the punishment of the villains. As is typical of the folktale, punishment is severe. There is no refinement of the kind introduced by Charles Perrault (1961), who has Cinderella embrace her torturers in the true spirit of Christianity. In the Jewish Moroccan versions the stepsister who posed as the prince's bride is put to death, her flesh roasted and sent to her mother. The mother believes that her daughter has sent her a gift and invites friends to share the meal with her. When she finally discovers the severed head of her daughter, she bursts into tears and bewails her death.

The Jewish Moroccan tale type is thus characterized by the following ten episodes, distinct from the five identified by Aarne and Thompson:

I. Instigated to murder by the woman who wants to marry her father, the heroine kills her mother.
II. The heroine convinces her father he should marry the other woman.
III. The heroine is persecuted (= AT 510 Ia, a$_1$).
IV. The magical help (= AT 510 II).
V. The heroine attends the ball (in contrast to AT 510 III).
VI. The heroine's true identity is recognized (= AT 510 IVa).
VII. The heroine marries the prince (= AT 510 V).
VIII. The heroine is injured and impersonated by the stepsister.
   (a) The heroine is turned into a dove.
   (b) The heroine is pushed into a well, or a room where dangers lurk.
IX. The heroine is saved.
   (a) As a result of her song, the needles are extracted and the heroine resumes her true identity.
   (b) As a result of the verses sung by the heroine and her

brother, the heroine is rescued.
X. The villains are punished.

As in the international tale type, the Smeda Rmeda type outlined above adheres to the pattern of maturation. Here, however, this pattern has merited extension beyond the marriage of the heroine. These narratives begin with the murder of the mother, move on to the father's remarriage, Smeda Rmeda's heroine's marriage to the prince, her apparent death, the birth of her child, and then conclude with the punishment of the wicked women. In the Jewish Moroccan folk narrative, female maturity is achieved when the woman has a child. This is, moreover, the reward of the woman who repents and suffers. The conclusion of this tale is an expression of poetic justice: the woman who made a girl kill her mother discovers the dismembered body of her daughter.

I have previously examined the story's morphology (Bar-Itzhak 1993). With the goal of uncovering its deep structure, the tale can also be studied using Claude Lévi-Strauss's structuralist approach.

Alan Dundes characterizes Levi-Strauss's approach as paradigmatic, that is, one in which the narrative material is reorganized into structural oppositions that are used to build a model of the narrative as whole (1968, xi-xii).[33] Levi-Strauss is aware of the importance of the different versions, regarding each as a system of substitutions relevant to analysis. Levi-Strauss does not begin by working on a group of narratives. Instead, he focuses on a single narrative, or "myth," which he examines for oppositions between certain qualities, and then attempts to rebuild the network of oppositions through which the local culture expresses itself.[34] His analysis is always immanent: details are regarded as essential, contributing to a model of structural oppositions within a tale.

Theoretically at least, the analyses done according to Levi-Strauss's approach seek to bridge the gap between the narrative and society:[35] the myth presents a microcosm of social relations. As the researcher focuses his attention on the concrete elements, he must remain in touch with the cultural environment, and ethnographic details may be noted, even if they do not occur in the narrative itself.

Using this structuralist approach, David Pace (1982) has attempted an analysis of an American Cinderella narrative collected from his students. Although I have my reservations about certain aspects of Pace's analysis,[36] I find that certain interesting conclusions suggest themselves when this approach is applied to the Jewish Moroccan versions. The structure of Freha Hafutah's version of the Smeda Rmeda narrative offers a good example.

The initial situation of the Smeda Rmeda tale involves two families:

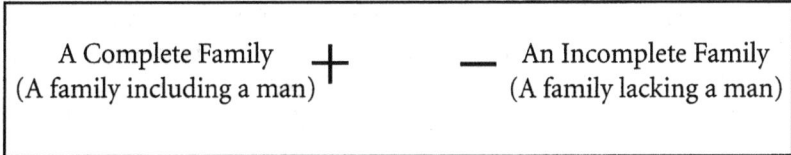

A Complete Family (A family including a man)	**+**	**—**	An Incomplete Family (A family lacking a man)	

Here, the incomplete family (the absence of a man) is understood to be in an inferior position vis-à-vis the complete one, and the situation must be remedied at all costs. The attempt to restore the family to completeness at the beginning of the story initiates a chain of oppositions between female characters:

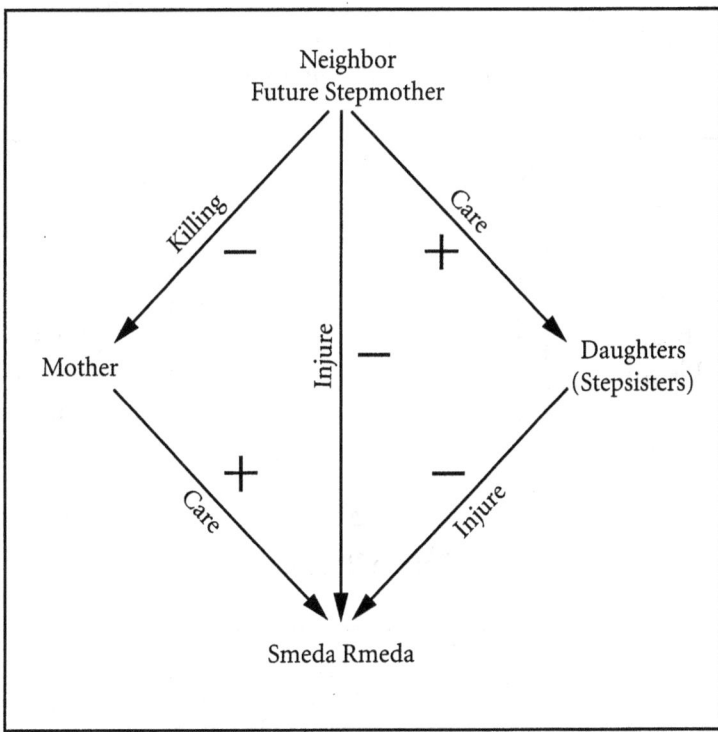

The network of oppositions revealed above highlights the centrality of blood relationships between women. In this narrative there is loyalty only where there is a blood relationship, and the absence of the bond of blood relationship results in enmity and hostility. Consequently, we understand to what extent the protagonist is at risk when she fails to be loyal to her mother. The mother's absence and the father's remarriage place the heroine in a family where nonconsanguinity isolates her and alters her status. Smeda Rmeda is thus reduced to the level of a servant, sleeping in the cook-room or the bakery, left in filth, and forced to do menial work at the mercy of the other women in the household.

A series of acts of mediation leads up to the final, corrected situation. These acts make it quite clear that women can be saved and redeemed only when a male figure steps in. This being so, the woman must take the initiative and act so as to merit deliverance at the hands of a man. For example, the stepmother actively seeks a husband for herself, and the other women in the narrative are equally active figures. Women in this tale act because they realize that men must be *made* to act, and because it is men, and only men, who can save and redeem them.

Initially, an opposition is established between the actions of Smeda Rmeda's stepmother and her father, as indicated below:

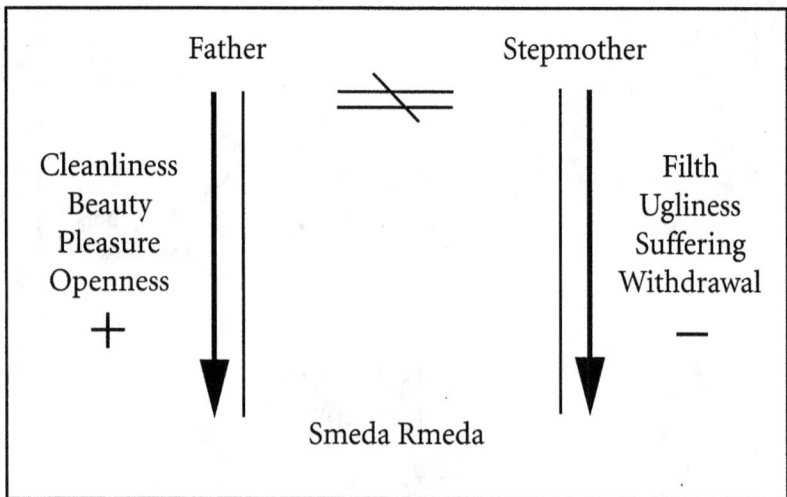

Father		Stepmother
Cleanliness		Filth
Beauty		Ugliness
Pleasure		Suffering
Openness		Withdrawal
+		−
	Smeda Rmeda	

The stepmother, who is liable to incur economic losses as well as loss of her daughters' preferential situation if Smeda Rmeda were to leave the household, tries to prevent the meeting of father and daughter. As Freha tells us, the father "rose and said to his wife: 'O my daughter, I will go to my daughter and ask her too what she wants.' 'Sit down, sit down,' said she to him, 'you just sit down. She is covered with soot and excrement all over, you have no reason to go and ask her.'" The stepmother thus tries to prevent the heroine from attending the ball, that is, from going out and from leaving the household altogether.

Although Smeda Rmeda knows the gifts to ask for (the nuts) and how to activate their magical properties, she clearly owes her initial, if temporary, deliverance to her father. The giant-demons that emerge from the walnuts, as all supernatural agents in Jewish Moroccan narratives, are also male. The father and magic help he provides enable the heroine to meet the prince (through the medium of the slipper) and to find a second state of deliverance.

As detailed earlier, the deliverance provided to Smeda Rmeda by her marriage to the prince concludes the European versions of the tale but is only temporary in the Jewish Moroccan versions. The second obstacle to Smeda Rmeda's happiness takes the form of an opposition between the actions of the prince and those of the stepmother:

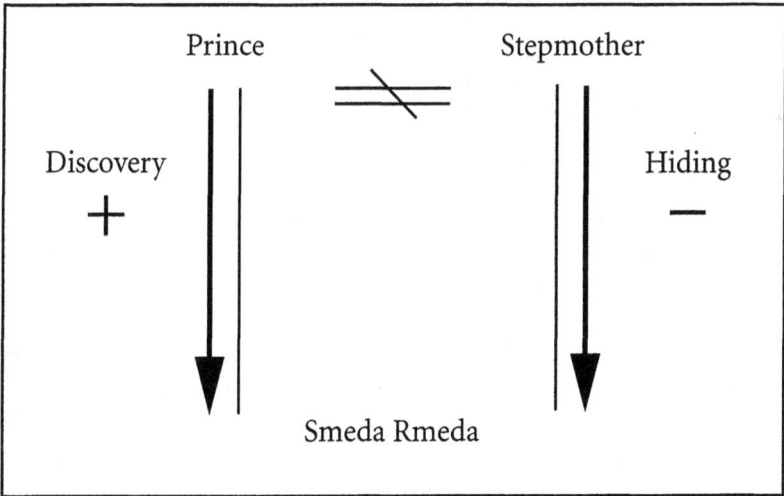

The older woman tries to hide the heroine from the prince, to arouse feelings of revulsion toward her by describing the filthy conditions in which she is living, and to prevent her from trying on the slipper. But Smeda Rmeda is saved from her stepmother by marriage to the prince, which offers a chance of social mobility and a change in status. Through marriage, the heroine is transformed from a girl into a woman; from filthy to clean; from ugly to beautiful; from the inhabitant of a cook-room to that of a palace; from endangered to protected.

As distinct from versions in which marriage represents final deliverance for the heroine, formal analysis demonstrates that as our narratives continue, a certain narrative function is repeated: namely, that of a woman causing injury to another woman in order to usurp her place alongside her husband. The stepmother instructs her daughter to find herself a husband at the expense of another woman, as the mother herself has done. To make up for what she lacks, the stepsister "kills" Smeda Rmeda, symbolically and occupies the position previously held by her. For the young characters, the situation reverts to what it was earlier in the plot, and the opposition between a married woman and an unmarried woman is reestablished. Early in the narrative, Smeda Rmeda violates the bond of female consanguinity, which represents the only loyalty possible between women. Here she once again trusts a woman who is not a blood relation (her stepsister), with similar results.

At this point in the narrative, Smeda Rmeda's father cannot help her, because she has passed from his control to that of her husband, and the prince believes the stepsister to be his wife. At this point Smeda Rmeda's stepsister has appropriated the protection of marriage for herself and has successfully deprived the heroine of her previous sources of male help. The brother, who was only a child in the first part of the narrative, resurfaces at this point, when the heroine cannot be rescued by the other male characters. In the traditional family in the Maghreb, the brother is in charge of his sisters and responsible for the honor of the family. He has the authority to punish them, and it is his obligation to kill his sister if her deeds bring shame upon her family. But it is also his duty to deliver her from danger and to come to her aid when she is threatened by outsiders. Smeda Rmeda's brother is the only remaining man who can protect her, and for this reason the stepsister tries to inflict injury upon him.[37] The stepsister realizes that unless the heroine's brother is killed, her position as the prince's wife will be in jeopardy.

Smeda Rmeda is saved because her brother's remarks arouse her husband's suspicions. However, what finalizes the heroine's deliverance and assures her status is not her marriage but the birth of her son. In Middle Eastern society a man is obligated as a blood relation to take care of his mother as long as she lives,[38] and thus the heroine's standing in the family is finally secure when she bears a son. The punishment of

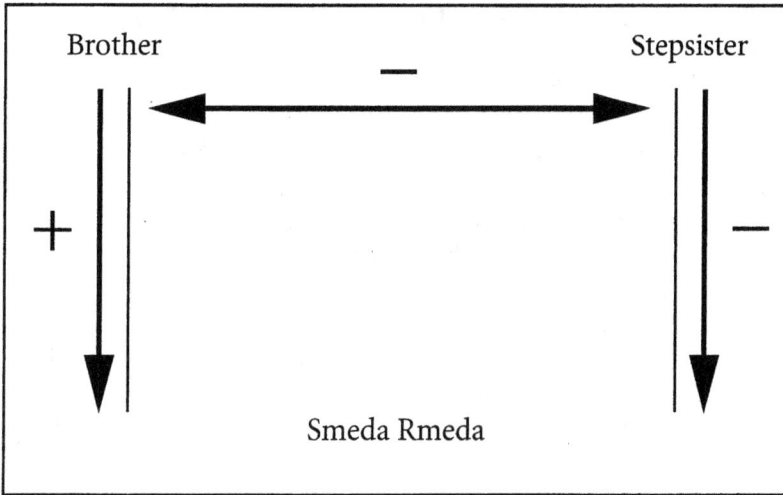

the villains at the end of the story is not only an expression of the insights acquired by the heroine regarding women who are not her blood relations, it is also an act of revenge that forestalls any future attacks: as Smeda Rmeda gains a child, the stepmother is punished by the loss of one. The correction finds expression in the situation at the end of the narrative:

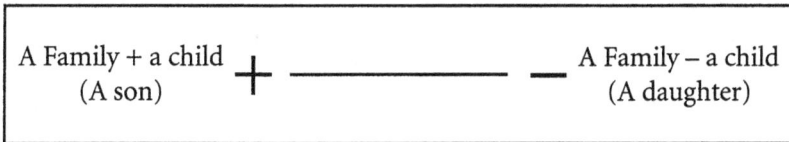

The reconstruction of oppositions and means of intermediation within the narrative enables us to understand the cultural language the narrator employs. We notice that the narrating society attaches importance to blood relationships, that men are perceived to possess the power to save and redeem women, and that such conditions shape the ways women relate to one another. In the Smeda Rmeda narrative, women are active, not victims of the "Cinderella syndrome" as it has been defined in feminist approaches to Western versions of the narrative. However, the activity of the women in the narrative does not undermine the prevailing patriarchal order of society but, conversely, affirms and reinforces it.

Structural analysis of this narrative supports the findings of contextual analysis of the storytelling event. Consider the declarative statement with which Freha prefaced her performance: "I am going to tell you a story my mother used to tell the family in order to teach the children to love their mother, avoid strange women trying to meddle with the lives of the family, and prefer family over friends." As suggested earlier, the addressees of Freha's message were her daughter and Avraham. At the time of the performance, the rest of the audience had no code with which to understand fully the significance of the tale.

An analysis of the story reveals its implicit cultural language. The reason for Freha Hafuta's choice in the particular conflict in which she finds herself becomes clear as well. Although Freha's distress is the result of her personal situation—her daughter's childlessness, her own old age and blindness—it is exacerbated by the transition to Israeli society and culture. Her daughter's living with a man without benefit of clergy is feasible in Israeli society, where this is not extraordinary, but is strongly censured in a town populated by Moroccan immigrants, most of them of the older generation. In reaction to her daily rebukes, the daughter and her partner shun the mother and even treat her with gross disrespect ("I don't listen to the nonsense of old people"). This would never have taken place back in Morocco, where respect for the parents' generation was a primary value.

In this situation Freha chooses the story of Smeda Remeda, the Jewish Moroccan Cinderella, because its underlying cultural language allows her to send a message related to her situation here and now. The importance of the blood tie between the women, and especially between mother and daughter, embedded in the deep structure of the story, can serve as a direct message to her daughter about her attitude toward her mother. Mainly, though, the story is aimed at the daughter's partner. The deep structure embodies a cultural statement that only a man can redeem and rescue a woman and provide her with a sheltered niche in society. This idea is addressed to Avraham. The narrator, perhaps afraid that the coded message will not be understood, also states it more explicitly in the concluding formula. In addition, the narrator's longing for her daughter to be rescued from her childlessness is expressed through the story's cultural code, according to which a woman's only fulfillment is bearing a son, because he will take care of her in her old age. But it is clear that such fulfillment can take place only after that which depends on her partner—namely, marriage.

In a situation of severe family crisis in Israel, a folktale that was frequently recounted by Jewish women in Morocco served to express frustration and to transmit a message that the narrator had proved unable to convey otherwise without creating a conflict with her family.

6

Ethnic Nonverbal Components
in the Jewish Moroccan Saints' Legend

Every culture is built of different systems of signs. Language and how it is used is a key element of every ethnic culture. Body language, including mimetic devices, gestures, and intonation, also characterizes and distinguishes an ethnic culture. In Israel, too, certain ethnic groups have become known for their distinctive body language, which has even become central to the popular stereotypes of members of some of these groups. But is there a body language characteristic of the saints' legends by Moroccan Jews? If so, it would be evidence of nonverbal communication as a criterion for defining a folk narrative genre.

For many years the study of the genre of folk narrative centered exclusively on textual-verbal aspects severing it from both context and performance. Aspects such as the narrative structure, the character, and the worldview served as criteria of genre definition and as means of genre delineation. Later studies reverse this approach, as shown by the thesis of Harold Sheub (1970, 119), who regards the narrative as performance only; as he puts it, narration is improvisational and original use of details and stylistic factors. The covert connection of the relations between the performer and the audience, and the mood of the artist—these fuse spatially and temporarily for a short period of time, and afterward only memory is left.

According to Bruce Rosenberg (1978, 150–51), a turning point in modern folklore research was reached with the acknowledgment of the humanist concept expressed in the anthropocentrism of various branches of study. The phrase that best stated this was "Becoming human is becoming unique" (Geertz 1973, 52). A perception of the world that placed the individual at its center caused a qualitative change of

153

emphasis in the study of folklore. The folklorists took up the concept presented in Milman Parry and Albert Bates Lord's work (1953–54) on Serbian poetry, which stressed the dynamic of the performer and the importance of the study of performance through awareness of personal talent. Interest thereupon came to focus on "parole" more than on "langue."

For purposes of this text, we can make use of the new definitions of the theatrical text that were added to the classic definitions dealing with content and dramatic structure of a text (that is, an occurrence consisting of a beginning, a middle, and an end whose vision is dynamic, requiring a response up to the climax and the denouement). I refer to the definitions of a theatric text as a system of signs and a communication system (Elam 1980). The theatric text in its performance aspect is defined by the semiotic method as a combination of various sign systems simultaneously directed to various channels of communication, that is, the ability to generate sentences deriving from various systems, such as the visual system, the auditory system, and so on. This links with the definition of the theatric text as a communication system with special addressor-addressee relations that derive from a multilayer system on various levels of communication operating simultaneously. As a result, the art of vocal expression, of gesture, and mimics have come under study. Expressive effects substituting for words, such as outbreaks, silences, mumbling, and expressions of surprise and pain have been examined, as well as characterization through changes in intonation or pronunciation, connection with music, audience appeal, and audience involvement as a stylistic device.

In his article on genre structure of Russian folklore, Vladimir Propp pointed out long ago that performance must be included with the criteria for the definition of the genres of folklore (1971, 232). Dan Ben-Amos proposes research along these lines while emphasizing definition by mode of performance (1975, 4). French folklorists dealing with African folklore have more specifically focused on this approach; mention must be made of Genevieve Calame-Griaule (1970) and especially of Gilbert Rouget. In a lecture delivered at the 1966 Congress of African Languages and Literature, Rouget spoke of the connection between certain texts and the use of certain vocal patterns as a criterion for the classification of African songs (1966).

The question to be examined here is whether nonverbal communication can serve as a criterion of genre definition of an ethnic folk narrative genre. The genre I chose in order to examine the nonverbal components of performance is the oral *Shevah* (praise) as told by Moroccan Jews. The *Shevah* narrative as defined by Yoseph Dan (1981, 82) is the narrative of a holy sanctified character, and according to him these narratives are distributed throughout the whole of traditional literature, folk literature, and historical homiletic and belles lettres. Dan distinguishes between "Shevah narratives" and "Sifrut Hashevahim," which he regards as a Hebrew parallel of the term "hagiography."

In international terminology the genre is called the Saints' Legend, or *Legende* in German. This terminology may seem problematic because of the Christian source—the Latin *Legenda,* namely, what was termed in church miraculous acts or acts of the saint. The Jewish Moroccan storytellers themselves term it the *ma'aseh.* In the course of my fieldwork I learned that the narrators used the term *ma'aseh* in ancient Hebrew, even though the language they normally spoke was Judeo-Arabic. In order to clarify the term and its meaning throughout the ages, it is necessary to study its usage in early Hebrew. In the Bible, *ma'aseh* is a noun too, but the meaning derives from the meaning of the verb, that is, what a person or God does, or the result of the doing. *Hazal* (the Sages of the Mishnah and the Talmud) attach three meanings to the word *ma'aseh,* the first of which coincides with the biblical meaning (Meir 1977, 4); the second meaning is "something that occurred, that happened, which is historic"; and the third is the *ma'aseh* as opposed to thought, theory, or precept. In the Mishnah, the term is frequently used in support of a religious precept or an argument. In all of these cases it is used in the sense of a fact anchored in reality, whose validity has been substantiated by evidence (Ginzberg 1961, IV, 54). In the Mishnah most *ma'asim* are short, they are confined to what is necessary in the context of the religious precept discussed, and their structure is: *ma'aseh,* query, and decision.

However, there is no doubt whether the term *ma'aseh* used by the narrators to designate the saints' legend is anchored in the ancient biblical usage indicating an action, something that is done, and the results of such action, because in the center of the saints' legend we have the action performed by the saint. But in the main the term is anchored in the meaning attached to it by *Hazal,* who regard the *ma'aseh* as grounded in history, something factual, the validity of which is supported by evidence. As the story of the saint is laid in historical time and place—and since the society narrating the narrative regards the events related by the narrative, including the supernatural occurrences, as truth (a fact conveyed by the narrative texts themselves)—it is no accident that the society adopted the term *ma'aseh* in its early sense, which carries this very meaning.

The saints' legend is a genre in whose center there is placed a character sanctified by the narrating society. The sanctity of the character in the Jewish saints' legend is a corollary of his close ties with God, as whose representative on earth he is regarded. He is the concretization of the amorphous Sacred Power and hence worthy of emulation; he is the mediator between God and the pious. Therefore, the saints' legend is an expression of religious experience within the folk society. By enabling folk-religious experience, the saints' legend meets people's need for a world of holiness and validates their system of folk-religious faith. A religious experience assumes the existence of a sacred world that is different in quality from the secular world. Human beings, deeds, and objects become valuable only when they take a share in the sacred world, and time, too, takes on a dimension of sacredness when the ritual is a reconstruction of events that occurred in the sacred past (Eliade 1959, 85–95). John J. Collins contends that expressions of religious experience include "Revelations," that is, personal encounters with the Sacred Power (1978, 29–52), and "Experienced Sympathy," according to Rodney Stark (1965, 99). The Sacred Power pays regard to an individual or to a group of individuals: the Power helps, performs miracles, or punishes. (Punishments, no less than help, imply that God is committed to watching over men's lives.) Expressions of religious experience also include myths and rituals and mystic experience. These turn into symbols of the Sacred Power, and therefore their observation conveys a sense of religious experience (Streng 1969, 66). In these the individual achieves a measure of communion with the Sacred Power.

The saints' legend has numerous poetic qualities.[1] Here, we will examine only the nonverbal aspects of performance.

Since the 1970s we have witnessed a return to the ethnocultural pattern of veneration of holy men and rituals connected with their tombs by many Israelis of Asian and North African origin (Ben-Ari and Bilu 1981; Yassif 1994, 506–29). When these Jews immigrated to Israel they were forced to leave behind the tombs of the holy men they had venerated in the "old country." This inaccessibility of course reduced the influence of such rituals. The immigrants were preoccupied with ensuring their survival and overcoming culture shock. Researchers from various academic disciplines have studied the problematics generated as a result of the encounter of Moroccan Jews with Israeli reality. The hardships of everyday life, the experience of the dominant Israeli culture, and the cultures of other ethnic groups have affected the society structure and the system of beliefs and opinions of the Jewish Moroccan ethnic culture in Israel.

A common phenomenon in the folk medicine of Moroccan Jews was the appeal to holy men to help people recover from illness. Such appeals to rabbis and holy men spawned many legends, which in turn further reinforced the custom. What has happened to these legends in Israel? An examination of the stories reveals a fascinating transformation in which the saints' legends build a bridge between the new environment and the beliefs brought from the old country, presenting the holy man in tandem with physicians so as to legitimize medical treatment without undercutting the old traditions.

Consider the following story, told by Nissim Malka, an immigrant from Morocco, as he heard it from Moshe Danino, also born in Morocco.

Many legends have been told about the wondrous righteous man Rabbi David U'Moshe, who worked miracles after his death. Most Jews from North Africa are willing to swear that the holy Rabbi David U'Moshe has appeared to them in a dream more than once—some say he appeared to them when they were awake—and granted their requests. In light of this many Jewish immigrants from North Africa have established synagogues and tombs for this miracle-working righteous man. They have done so in Jaffa and Sefad, in Ashqelon and Ofaqim, and perhaps in other places as well.

To this day many devotees of this holy man stream to prostrate themselves on his monuments throughout the country, and elsewhere, to pray for the fulfillment of their wishes. Often their wishes are granted.

Moshe Danino, who built a synagogue and monuments in memory of the righteous man next to his house, recounts many of his wonders. Danino will swear to the truth of the following story.

Once his wife, Sarah, fell seriously ill. The doctors told him that she had to undergo a brain operation that might perhaps save her life.

In light of the danger Danino refused to risk his wife's life and began to moan plaintively in the synagogue he had built in memory of the holy man.

He cried out bitterly: "Know, Rabbi David U'Moshe, that if you don't save my wife I will no longer believe in your greatness."

Suddenly Danino heard a voice speaking to him: "My son, take your wife to the physicians. With God's help no harm will befall her, for I will be with her."

When the woman was wheeled to the operating room, even before the doctors put her to sleep, with her own eyes she suddenly saw the holy man standing alongside her and the doctors.

An operation of the type performed on Sarah, even when it is successful, frequently causes the patient to lose his or her sight, partially or completely. But Sarah came through the surgery successfully and recovered fully from her illness as if she had never been ill.

The doctors believe that she is the first woman ever to undergo this dangerous procedure with such success.

The doctors asked Moshe Danino, Sarah's husband, what his wife had done. He replied: "She is simply a God-fearing woman and has strong faith in the miracles performed by righteous men."

The pious Moshe Danino did not reveal the secret of the righteous man Rabbi David U'Moshe, who had appeared to him and told him what to do.
(IFA 12337)

This story presents the dilemma of the change being experienced by the community, from traditional modes of healing to the patterns of Israeli medicine, and which finds acute expression precisely in crises of serious illness. After hearing the doctors' opinion that his wife must undergo brain surgery to save her life, the hero addresses a prayer for deliverance to the holy man whom he venerates. His defiant challenge of "if you don't save my wife I will no longer believe in your greatness" also expresses the dilemma of whether he should continue to maintain the hallowed beliefs of the past or cast them aside.

But the story shows that the members of the community have rejected a radical solution in favor of a sort of synthesis of the two worlds. The hero brings his wife for surgery, accepting the need to rely on modern medicine, but does so because the holy man appeared to him and told him to do so.

The doctors perform the operation, but the cultural exegesis of their success is that the holy man was standing next to them. The fact that the woman does not lose her sight, as usually happens after such operations, receives the cultural explanation that this was a miracle wrought by the holy man.

Nevertheless, the coda of this story—"the pious Moshe Danino did not reveal the secret of the righteous man Rabbi David U'Moshe, who had appeared to him and told him what to do"—points out the estrangement between the two worlds in Israeli culture. The narrating culture manages to find the golden mean between modern medicine and its belief in holy men without infringing upon that belief; but it is aware of the fact that this will not be viewed favorably by the hegemonic culture. Consequently it remains a sort of cultural code internal to the community, which must not be revealed to outsiders. It also serves to express a sense of superiority: only *we* know the secret, the true reason for the doctors' success. This feeling is certainly an expression of the cultural and personal needs of a traditional ethnic society in a changing world.

In the course of my fieldwork with Moroccan Jews I recorded seventy-one performances of narratives that belong to the genre of saints' legend both on grounds of textual research criteria and according to ethnic genre criteria applied by the narrators themselves.[2] I found that all the narratives have the same nonverbal aspects of performance, which enables assigning them to the same genre. In the findings presented here I do not relate to specific modes of performance of individual narrators unless these latter apply to other narrators too, because my objective was not the study of the fundamentals of performance relative to the artist, but relative to the genre. (At the same time, it is obvious that essentially identical performance has various shades of difference depending on the personality traits of individual narrators.) In the communication process of narration of the folk narrative, the relationship between the narrator and the listeners creates the folk narrative text. Therefore I have analyzed below the visual and auditory effects of both the narrator and his audience during the performances of saints' legends.

Visual Effects of the Narrator
- Kissing of hand and hand touching eyes whenever the saint's name is mentioned.
- Rhythmic swaying of body as the plot of the narrative unfolds. (Motion is discontinued and resumed with direct speech or at the end of an episode.)

- Closing eyes to express piety (in sections of the narrative where the saint is revealed, heals, helps, or punishes).
- Facial expression of secrecy when the practice of the saint that brings about the miracle is disclosed, the verbal report of which is encoded, for example, "He did whatever he did," "He said whatever he said."
- Kissing the book containing the saints' legends (especially *Shevah Haim* by Mazal Makhluf Tarim).[3] Narrators in possession of this book would display it, kiss it, and with the closed book in front of them, would narrate a narrative, claiming that it was from this book.

Visual Effects of the Audience

- Kissing of hand and hand touching eyes whenever the saint's name is mentioned or when the narrator uses the same effect.
- Expressing piety and elation in passages where the saint is revealed, heals, helps, or punishes, or when the tomb of the saint is referred to as a place of pilgrimage.
- Expressing knowledge of a secret when the narrator reports the practice of the saint that leads to the miracle. (When the narrator says, "He did what he did," his knowledge of the secret is transmitted to the audience—they received the secret message, and this is unmistakably reflected in their facial expression.)
- Kissing of the book by the listeners (in case the narrator brings the book along when he tells the narrative).

Auditory Effects of the Narrator

- Expressive effects instead of complete words—mumbling (frequently of prayers or blessings).
- Intonation games—intonation of a secret code when the practice of the saint is narrated, which leads to the miraculous occurrence.
- Absence of change of intonation in connection with the delineation of a character—there is no imitation and no mimicry. While in other genres one of the outstanding features is change of intonation when the narrator moves from one character to another (which sometimes makes for comic effects, e.g., when a man—the narrator—mimics the voice of a woman, or wails like a woman), this device is never used in the saints' legend, the implication being that a high level of seriousness is maintained throughout—there is no room for any deviation whatsoever.

Storyteller Mordekhai Malka performing a saints' legend (Courtesy of
Israel Folktale Archives)

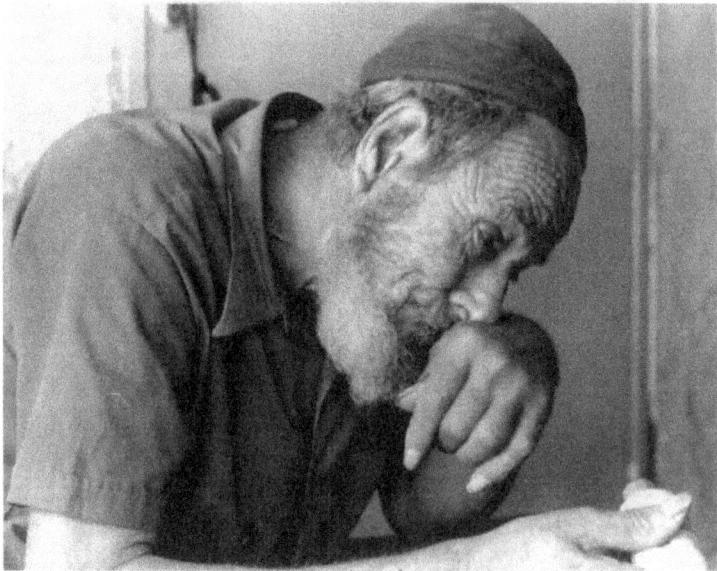

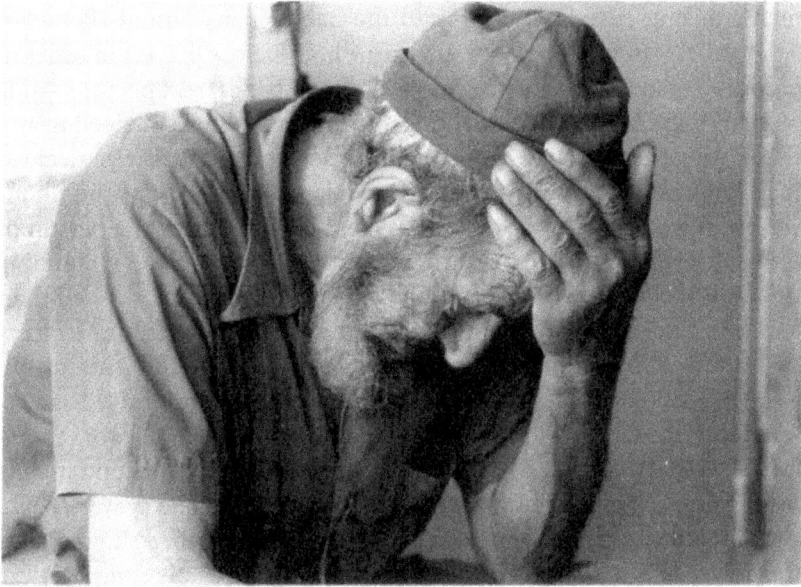

Auditory Effects of the Audience
- Mumbling (a blessing, a prayer, Amen).
- Confirmation of the miracle performed. This reinforces the belief in the narrative (e.g., Ah! Aha!); it may lead to explicit verbal reassurance and to a new narrative told by another narrator.

The visual and auditory effects embedded in this genre link with the world of holiness of the narrating society—with the synagogue and the worshippers. The use of body language as part of religious worship existed in pagan societies and has continued to exist in monotheistic religions. Judaism, too, connects prayer with body language. Devoutness is known as an element of the worship of God, and in particular of prayer. Kissing is a feature of sacred worship—kissing the Torah or the fringed garment worn by pious Jews (*Tzizit*). The practice of swaying the body during prayer sessions and even to set it in motion by pacing up and down, jumping, or other movement, as the Psalmist says: "All my bones shall say, Lord, who is like unto thee?" (Psalms 35:10) existed as early as the *Tanaim* (the Sages of the Talmud), and it was said of Rabbi Akiva that when someone left him as he was praying, and then returned, he would find that the rabbi had taken a different posture. In the Middle Ages, too, this was known to be a typically Jewish practice

(Ha'levi 1984, 2, 20). *Hazal* made rules for the posture and body movements during prayer. According to the Babylonian Talmud (Berachot 5a), the first Hasidim would wait for one hour before prayers in order to become attuned to them. The legs must be in the correct posture—side by side (Berachot 10b) and the body upright except when kneeling and rising when God's name is mentioned (Berachot 12a). It was decided that the words of prayer must be articulated with the lips, but, conversely, it was said that he who raises his voice in prayer is a person of little faith (Berachot 24a), and therefore the prayer *Amidah* ("Standing up") was recited in whispers. In ancient times, worshippers raised their hands in prayer and apparently spread their fingers. After the Destruction of the Temple, this practice was discontinued, and only the custom of raising hands when reciting the blessing of Kohanim survived as a reminder of the custom; it was decided that when praying, the worshipper must "wring his hands" (Babylonian Talmud, Shabbat 10a) and incline his head (Babylonian Talmud, Rosh Ha'shana 26b). The prayer *Nefilat Apayim* ("Prostration") was recited by each individual worshipper after the prayer *Amidah*, which was recited jointly by the whole congregation. Today, the text of this prayer is definitive and there is no room for spontaneity, but its character of "prostration" has been preserved inasmuch as the body is either inclined or actual prostration takes place. The rabbinic authorities generally prohibited prostration on the ground with arms and legs outstretched.

Concerning the swaying motion of the body, I found some interesting ethnic evidence in one of the narratives of the sample (IFA 7192). The narrative deals with a preacher who comes on the Sabbath to preach in the synagogue. The whole congregation pleads with him, asking him to wait for Rabbi Haim Pinto, who is late. Finally the rabbi arrives, and the preacher preaches. When the sermon is over, the congregation, who accompany the preacher, are stunned when they see that the preacher boards a ship and starts smoking. When they tell Rabbi Haim Pinto what happened, he replies: "'An inner voice warned me, and I did not want to come and listen to the sermon, and when I came I saw that he was not a Jew.' 'And how did you know?' asked the townsmen. 'When he stood there and preached his sermon, I noticed that he stood up straight and did not sway his body, I understood that he is not a Jew, for a Jew has a soul, and when he preaches he sways,' replied Rabbi Pinto."

The visual and auditory effects that constitute the basic elements of performance of the genre are thus ecstatic elements used by the narrator to carry away the audience, who participate in a folk–religious experience. Here the performance unites with the textual essence. In the center of the genre there is a human character sanctified by the narrating society. His sanctity derives from the normative religious sacred power. The character is an object of veneration and emulation who in the society serves as a medium of religious identification. In the genre, the narrator uses holy language not only in the textual-verbal sense, but also on the level of nonverbal signs of communication. He chooses his signs from gestures, mimics, and sounds from the central world of holiness— prayer and the synagogue—and carries away his audience in an ecstatic experience involving the sum total of all channels of communication.

As regards the Jewish Moroccan narrators and audiences, the nonverbal aspects of performance are so striking and typical of the genre that they can serve as criteria for genre definition even in the absence of a verbal text. A study of the performance elements of body language can be used to investigate cultural processes within an ethnic group. From this we can learn about patterns of continuity and change in the ethnic culture in Israel vis-à-vis the culture of the country of origin. We can also learn about the complex of relations between the older generation, the bearers of the past tradition, and the younger generation that grew up in Israel and were educated in the Israeli school system.

Most of the situations in which I recorded saints' legends were in the homes of the narrators. All of the auditory and visual elements of narrator and audience mentioned above were characteristic of the older generation. Some members of the younger generation who were present echoed in the nonverbal elements, while others did not. But I never encountered negative reactions toward this body language in any of the performances in the narrators' own homes.

One performance outside the narrators' homes took place in the community center in Shelomi. I had organized a get-together of elderly narrators whom I had met during my fieldwork, which at the time had been going on for nearly a year. I also invited students and research fellows from the university. When we arrived at the community center, we encountered a large group of local young people who were wandering about with nothing to do. We told them about the meeting and invited them to join us and listen to the stories, which they did. The adults told stories one after another, and at a certain point one of them began telling a saints' legend. When he mentioned the saint's name he made the characteristic gesture of kissing the hand. The older listeners made the same gesture, but the young locals did not. Instead, they began to giggle and laugh, while looking at the university students in the audience. The researchers and students did not imitate the gesture, but listened seriously and attentively to the story.

As the story progressed, we witnessed a change in the behavior of the local young people. As the plot thickened, the giggles and snickers died down. By the end of the story, most of the young people were mimicking the gestures of the narrator and old people every time the saint's name was mentioned. Their body language also reflected the other gestures typical of the narrator and older members of the audience.

The fact that the giggles and snickers that accompanied the start of the story were not observed when the young people were present at storytelling events at home indicates that they are more comfortable with manifestations of the ethnic culture within their affinity group than in a mixed audience that includes those whom they view as representative of the hegemonic Israeli culture. The reaction of the young people to the body language used with the genre shows that at least for some of these youths, their affinity group no longer serves fully as their reference and identification group. One may conjecture that this is also associated with absorption policy at the time of the mass waves of immigration and the melting-pot ideology that aimed at eliminating the previous ethnic cultures and creating a uniform culture to facilitate rapid integration of the multiple diasporas. I have dealt with this point at length in my discussion of immigration and absorption stories.

The fact that the young people modified their behavior as the story went on points to the power of the saints' legend, the folk genre associated with the sanctified world of beliefs, to serve as a medium for creating identification with the ethnic culture and its values even when the hegemonic culture rejects and sometimes denigrates the values of the home culture. The young people's return to the body language of the world of holiness, typical of the genre, attests to this better than a thousand witnesses.

Notes

Chapter 1

1. Told by Yehudit Tsoref (IFA 22863).
2. In 1957 PICA closed its accounts with the settlers, transferred all of its property to the State of Israel, and conveyed an area of 130,000 *dunams* to the Jewish National Fund. Over the years, the Rothschild family and ICA/PICA have invested approximately £5.5 million in the settlement of Eretz Israel.
3. For a discussion of sacred narratives accompanied by an exposition of various approaches, see Dundes 1984.
4. Told by Yehudit Tsoref (IFA 22863).
5. In Spanish, the name is *Azufaifo;* French, *Jujubier;* Italian, *Giugalo;* and in Greek, *Tjtjifia.* In Christian tradition the plant is known as "Christ's thorn." For further information, see Mabberley 1981, 624–25.
6. Most kibbutzim have documented their histories almost from their founding. Almost every kibbutz has its own archives. The ample archives of Kibbutz Gennosar were of great assistance to my research.
7. Tsoref 1964, 51–61.
8. "Yisrael" is Yisrael Levy, one of the founders of the kibbutz and one of its most dominant and admired figures. He was killed in battle during the War of Independence.
9. This refers to a group of members who were arrested after a brawl with Arabs from the neighboring village, in which one of the villagers was killed.
10. Bar-Gal and Shammai refer to a similar phenomenon in other places of modern colonization and settlement, accompanied by contact between human beings and the landscape—for instance, the United States and New Zealand. See, for example, Lawson and Stockton 1981, 527–35; Watson 1971, 65–77.
11. This is not the place for a discussion of the exegesis of these verses. Many interpretations have been heaped on the words rendered in the text as "are trees of the field human[?]" (1985 Jewish Publication Society translation). Various midrashim and exegetes present this meaning, while others view the clause as stating that human life is associated with and depends on trees.

12. For further discussion of Judaism's attitude toward trees, see, for example, Patai 1942, Ayali 1995.
13. The jujube plays an important role in Arab folklore. A Moslem legend tells of a jujube tree that has as many leaves as there are human beings. On the fifteenth day of the month of Ramadan some of its leaves fall off; every one of them corresponds to a person who will die in the coming year (Dafni 2004). In another version of the story, this particular jujube is said to be growing in Paradise (ibid.).

  The jujube also plays an important role in Palestinian Arab folklore. The tree is considered to be sacred. When it reaches the age of forty, the *walim* (righteous men) sit beneath it (ibid.). Someone who has the temerity to cut down a righteous man's jujube brings down destruction on his head. The Palestinian Arabs accord a great respect to the jujube. I would like to thank Amotz Dafni for allowing me to read his unpublished article, "The Common Jujube: The Tree of the Seventh Heaven." On the jujube in Palestinian folk tales, see also Muhawi and Kanaana 1988, 122–25.
14. Told by Shulke Lupan (IFA 22835).
15. Told by Yovi Lupan as he heard from Moshe Abas (IFA 22836).
16. Told by Benny Lupan (IFA 22837).
17. Told by Noa Kaplan (IFA 22838).
18. Told by Noa Kaplan (IFA 22839).
19. There are two kinds of Montpellier snakes—the Malpolon Moilensis and the Malpolon Monspessulanus. Some of the Montpellier snakes are poisonous and some are not.
20. Two stories of Yovi Lupan (IFA 22840 and IFA 22841).
21. The recording was done by my student Rachel Duzzy.
22. Told by Noa Kaplan (IFA 22843).
23. On the importance of context in folklore research, see Ben-Amos 1971, 3–15; 1993, 209–26.
24. Told by Iris Kritz (IFA 22864).
25. In 1997 I gave a lecture at Stanford University on this subject. One of the participants wrote to his brother, who is a member of Kibbutz Shomrat, about the Gennosar narrative. He sent me his response via e-mail: "The vatikim [old-timers] on Shomrat did the same to an olive grove in order to plant oranges. A stupid move by any stretch of the immigration. I take great pleasure in being the one who is replanting Olive trees in the same area where the Olive trees were" (Y. B., personal communication, January 1997).
26. Summarizing symbols are symbols that "sum up, express, [and] represent for the participants in an emotionally powerful and relatively undifferentiated way what the system means to them" (Ortner 1973, 1339–40).

Chapter 2

1. The Labor Brigade, or to give it its full name, the "Joseph Trumpeldor Labor and Defense Brigade," was a pioneering organization established at a memorial meeting for Joseph Trumpeldor held in 1920 after he was killed defending Tel Hai. The founders, veterans of the *Halutz* group in Russia, were comrades and students of Trumpeldor. The brigade's objective was to build the Land of Israel on socialist foundations and get it ready for mass immigration by setting up a countrywide commune composed of settlement groups and labor detachments, with a common purse and equality of living conditions for all members. The brigade established a network of agricultural and urban detachments and penetrated every branch of activity—paving roads, draining swamps, construction, agriculture, crafts and light industry, and public works. All income was turned over to the common purse, which provided for the needs of all members.

2. Emmanuel Sivan, in his reference to losses of the kibbutz movement during the War of 1948, says: "If one looks at the kibbutz movement as a reservoir of the 'serving elite,' the latter has indeed paid a big price in blood as expected of a rank of this kind" (1991, 121).

3. In Hebrew, the words "air" and "atmosphere" derive from the same root, hence there is wordplay here.

4. The Palmach was a prestate military organization formed by the Haganah high command in 1941 in response to the threat of Nazi invasion of Palestine.

5. The term "myth" does not imply a negative evaluation of the narrative as either false or invalid, but rather highlights its sacred character in the culture under study.

6. I recorded five versions of the following story narrated by Yair Benari in different narrative situations. I possess two additional versions that were recorded by others. This story was told in a meeting in Benari's house.

7. In referring to the memorial literature of the fallen in battle in 1948, Emmanuel Sivan shows how the concept of "binding" becomes central to this literature and points to similar characteristics to those revealed in Lavie's story—fighting activism of the victim and the changing of the goal for which the sacrifice is needed (1991, 201).

8. Regarding the ambivalent attitude of the parental generation to the next generation of Sabras, compare Sivan 1991, 56–100.

9. In Hebrew, the word *lihbosh* can mean both "to conquer" or "to tread down a road or a path."

10. Yair Benari and other informants in the kibbutz told me many stories about Moshe Carmi. These stories emphasize his contribution in imparting knowledge of the Bible, geography of the Land of Israel, and nature excursions to the children of Ein Harod.

11. Sivan indicates the same phenomenon in the memorial literature to the fallen of the War of Independence. The past critics criticize their criticism and praise the uniqueness of this generation (1991, 50–60).

12. These are the names of the two kibbutzim after the split on ideological ground occurred in the 1950s.

13. It is interesting to note that recently a public debate has arisen in Israel concerning the propriety of the media's publication/broadcast of photographs of soldiers in tears at the funeral of their fallen comrades. Some assert that such photos provide aid and comfort to terrorists and allow them to exult at the success of their attacks on Israeli soldiers. Although this argument has been rejected in the main, and the general public is in favor of showing expressions of emotion, there is no debate that this doubt exposes how much values have altered from the worldview expressed in the remarks of Atara Shturman, which was predominant in Israeli society during the prestate period and in the first decades after independence.

14. Joseph Trumpeldor (1880–1920) was a soldier and pioneer who was killed defending Tel Hai. His life and death became a symbol of bravery and self-sacrifice in the service of the homeland.

Part 2 Introduction

1. For an exhaustive treatment of the subject, see Wilson 1989, 21–37.

2. Georges lists the studies by R. B. Klymasz (1980) and B. S. Weinreich (1960) as studies of this kind.

3. *Mizrahim* or *Edot ha'mizrah*, literally "the orientals" or "the oriental ethnic groups," are terms for Jews from North Africa and Asia.

Chapter 3

1. This was part of the tendency to Judaize the Galilee. (See Kipnis 1983, 723–24; Rabinowitz 1996, 6–7.)

2. Despite this fact, an information sheet put out by the Upper Nazareth municipality in 1984 states that "the first settlers came to the Nazareth hills at the beginning of 1957. Most of them were veteran Israelis—managers, military personnel, and others who wanted to participate in the establishment of a new and developing community." This reflects the Israeli official policy toward the status of new immigrants.

3. On homiletical derivations in Jewish ancient culture and in the folklore of Polish Jews, see Bar-Itzhak 2001, 27–44.

4. The attempt to establish the formal text of the folktale is best known from the work of Vladimir Propp (1968). His method differentiates between contents and form and establishes a division into two categories, one

variable and the other fixed. On the plane of each individual narrative there are the characters and their actions, and these may change from one story to another. The analytic level is the fixed formal level. On this level reside the narrative roles and their functions, which are abstract, general, and unchanging.

5. Told by Yosef Goldman (IFA 22849).
6. For a different attitude to Jewish humor, see Ben-Amos 1973, 112–31.
7. Told by Moniek Zand (IFA 22850).
8. Since the early years of statehood a national absorption policy was elaborated, one of its chief architects being David Ben-Gurion. In Ben-Gurion's formulation, the purpose of statehood was to facilitate the cultural absorption of the immigrants; it was to expedite the process of "blending" of the returning exiles through a set of values and symbols that laid emphasis on what the different population groups had in common and that hallowed the principles of national unity and state sovereignty (Bar-Itzhak and Shenhar 1993a, 128–29).
9. For an interesting ethnography of Upper Nazareth in the 1990s that reflects a very different worldview, see Rabinowitz 1996.
10. Told by Ya'akov Goldberg (IFA 22851).

Chapter 4

1. In the 1950s Dov Noy established the Israel Folktale Archives (IFA) and together with students and volunteers started an intensive collection of folk narratives from storytellers from different ethnic groups in Israel, among them the Yemenite Jews. The IFA is located at the University of Haifa, and today includes 23,000 folk narratives, of which 1,588 were recorded from Yemenite Jews in Israel. This is the third ethnic group in size that is represented in the archives, after Polish Jewry (2,807 narratives) and Moroccan Jewry (2,065 narratives).
2. The process of change of the language of the narrative was exhaustively treated by Hasan-Rokem in 1982.
3. Discussions of acculturation can be found in most of the notes and studies published in the volumes of the IFA. Also see Shtal 1970.
4. Rabbi Shalom Shabazi was born in 1619, when Yemen was under Turkish rule. He was a great Jewish Yemenite poet. In 1679, the Imam Ahmed Iben Hassan Iben Alkassem expelled the Jews from Sanna and central Yemen, and they had to move to Muz'a, a deserted area in Haramauth on the coastal plain of the Red Sea in western Yemen. Shabazi was sixty when the Jews were expelled. Thereafter nothing is known about him except for the fact that he was buried in Ta'ez. Cf. Tobi 1972, Hoze 1973, Bar-Itzhak 1987. On Rabbi Shalom Sharabi, see Alendaf 1928, Sorski 1974, and Gafner 1970, 31–50.

5. Told by Shlomo Beit-Ya'acov (IFA 12099).
6. Told by Mazal Ben-Ami (IFA 13006).
7. Told by Yosef Haim Kiruani (IFA 6448).
8. Told by Nissim Hibba (IFA 9823).
9. See, for example, Lewis 1989, Gilad 1989.
10. Kirshenblatt-Gimblett coined the term "culture shock" in connection with folkloristic creativity in times of crisis. In her investigations of Eastern European Jewish immigrants to Canada she refers to the period of immigration as a period of culture shock that is conducive to folkloristic creation. In another publication (Kirshenblatt-Gimblett 1983, 38–47) she proposes special guidance to fieldwork with immigrants that stresses, among other things, the transition period in the new country (ibid., 41).
11. Told by Yona Seri (IFA 6031). Published in Seri 1968, no. 8.
12. When discussing the legends about Rabbi Shalom Shabazi, Noy constructed a biographical scheme of the life of the saint based on the times when the events occurred in the saint's life (1967; 1977). See also Bar-Itzhak 1987.
13. Yemenite Jews used amulets to protect the lives of babies, as was shown by Yoseph Kapach (1961, 163–67).
14. In other words, he should make a pilgrimage to the synagogue named for Shabazi's name.
15. Bashari was the man who built the synagogue.
16. Told by Sara Erez (IFA 13434).
17. An investigation of the biographical scheme in the legends about Rabbi Shalom Shabazi revealed that 52 percent of the narratives are set in the period after his death (Bar-Itzhak 1987, 192).
18. Told by Batia Hadad (IFA 13432).
19. Told by Batia Hadad (IFA 13442).
20. For personal narrative and memorate, see, for example, Honko 1964, Dègh and Vazsonyi 1974, Dolby-Stahl 1989.

Part 3 Introduction

1. According to the Israel Central Bureau of Statistics, 984,568 immigrants arrived in the country between 1948 and 1960.
2. Between 1965 and 1979, 161,864 immigrants reached Israel from the Soviet Union. Between 1990 and 1998, 755,000 immigrants arrived from the (former) Soviet Union. Only 473 immigrants came from Ethiopia before 1980. About 17,000 arrived in the 1980s, including 6,700 in Operation Moses, a series of flights from the Sudan in November and December 1984. Another 37,000 came in the 1990s, including 14,000 in Operation Solomon, a weekend airlift in May 1991.

Chapter 5

1. For a detailed report on my fieldwork in Shelomi, see Bar-Itzhak and Shenhar 1993.
2. Most of the women whose stories we transcribed in Shelomi did not know their exact date of birth.
3. During the two years that I met with Haviva Dayan, I never once saw her sitting idle. Even when she was telling stories she kept her hands busy sewing lovely pillow covers from scraps of fabric.
4. According to our informants, *Alaguz* is a term used in Judeo-Arabic language when referring to an old woman.
5. Couscous is a traditional Moroccan dish prepared with semolina.
6. The narrator is referring to the muezzin who calls Muslims to morning prayers.
7. Halama is a legendary place.
8. According to folk belief, love and hatred are located in the liver. When a loved one is harmed, the liver undergoes a change, as though it is burned. In Arabic there is a metaphor to express the wish that no harm should come to the beloved—that is, that his liver should not be burned. In Hebrew as well there are expressions that reflect the folk belief that feelings are located in inner parts of the body such as kidneys and heart. God is characterized as *Bohen Klayot Va'lev*—"He who sees what is in the kidneys and hearts of people."
9. IFA 10094, from Greece, was published in Attias 1976, no. 7; IFA 5528, from Libya, was published in Noy 1967, no. 63; IFA 12503, from Turkey, was published in Alexander and Noy 1989, no. 63.
10. In creating a performance-centered text, I have been inspired by Elizabeth Fine's suggestions (1984). However, the uniqueness of the event has necessitated some changes. As Fine herself claims, "Each folklore performance, as a unique artistic experience, presents unique problems, which cannot be solved by a mechanical application of rules. . . . [I]t seems dubious that a universal application or text style will meet the demands of the many and varied folklore performances" (1984, 149–50). As the following pages illustrate, I have adhered to Fine's suggested format in some ways and altered it in others. This narrative is stored in the Israel Folktale Archives (IFA 16445).
11. The narrator is addressing the women to whom she is telling the tale.
12. *Barkuksh* is a dish cooked with semolina and milk and served with butter.
13. *Kappara* is an expiatory sacrifice: "I am prepared to let my life be an expiatory sacrifice for you" would be an expression of love.
14. This phrase is a typical connector in Jewish Moroccan storytelling.
15. That is to say, the whole population came, even the poorest and the ugliest.

16. Samsam-Kamkam is a gigantic demon, sometimes called Samsam ben Kamkam, usually described as "having his head in the sky and his feet in the water."

17. The narrator blesses the listeners.

18. However, it should be noted that there is one Judeo-Moroccan narrative in the IFA (IFA 6859, collected by Billy Kimchi from Esther Alzara Arpood of Ma'alot) that belongs to Cox's types B and C, Rooth's type B1, and AT 510 B ("The Golden Dress, the Money, and the Stars"). In this version, the character of Smeda Rmeda is not mentioned, and, as in the international type, the protagonist is a princess.

19. A recording of this version may be found in the IFA (IFA 8595).

20. This version and a discussion of it are included in *Cinderella: A Folklore Casebook* (Dundes 1982, 3–13).

21. Apart from the Moroccan narratives, there are sixteen Jewish parallels from Islamic countries in the IFA: Tunis (2), Turkey (1), Lebanon (1), Sephardic Israel (1), Yemen (2), Iraqi Kurdistan (2), Persian Kurdistan (2), Iraq (1), Bukhara (3), Mghanistan (1). See also Alexander 1994.

22. The version collected by Margaret Mills in Iran, which she claims is characteristic of both Iran and Afghanistan, contains narrative stages similar to those found in the Jewish Moroccan versions: an opportunistic teacher at a religious school questions one of her students, the daughter of a trader, about her family's financial status. When the widowed teacher discovers that the family is well-off, she asks the girl what provisions they have at home. The girl tells her they have vinegar, whereupon the widow convinces her student of her good intentions and that the girl's mother is wicked. She then suggests that the girl should ask her mother to get her some vinegar and that she should push her mother into the vessel in which the vinegar is stored and close it. The girl does so, and after some time the father marries the schoolteacher. When the teacher has a daughter of her own, she begins to mistreat her stepdaughter (1982, 185–89).

23. According to my informants, the word *Smeda* means a fine semolina, used to prepare couscous. *Rmeda* derives from the word *Rmad,* meaning ashes.

24. According to my informants, this is a frightful demon. *Samsam* means odorous, and *Kamkam* means eating or devouring. Although the name of this demon is applied to persons who inspire fear, Smeda Rmeda controls the demon, and therefore he serves her.

25. Many proverbs compare a man who moves from one woman to another to a person who changes shoes or socks frequently (Bettelheim 1977, 267–71).

26. The narrative detail of the small shoe is believed to be of Oriental origin (cf. Waley 1947).

27. This is a variation of AT 403 W, "The Substituted Bride," as discussed later.

28. The blindness of this stepsister recalls the Grimms' version, which concludes with the punishment of the stepsisters by the birds pecking out their eyes.

29. Smeda Rmeda's transformation into a dove in these versions recalls the doves and fairy-doves in some of the European versions of the tale.

30. A comparable motif occurs in the Grimms' version, where tar is used to catch Aschenputtel as she attempts to leave the party before the wedding.

31. This is Motif D154.1 (a human being is turned into a dove), and a variation of AT 405, "Jorinde and Joringel" (in which a girl is magically transformed into a bird, and a young man uses a spell to restore her to her true form).

32. Also indexed as Motif K191.1 (the false bride dresses as the true bride, occupies her place without the bridegroom's knowledge, and harms the bride).

33. Whereas the surface structure of the story is syntagmatic, that is, governed by temporal and causal principles, the deep structure is paradigmatic, based on static logical relations among the elements.

34. His study of myth assumes that the structure underlying every myth is that of a four-term homology, correlating one pair of opposed mythemes with another (Levi-Strauss 1963, 20–31).

35. An innovative approach to the relation of reality and art has been suggested by Galit Hasan-Rokem (1988, 75).

36. As Dundes has pointed out, Pace identifies the Cinderella narrative as a "myth" (Dundes 1982, 246). Moreover, it is not clear whether Pace is referring to each of his students' versions as an individual "text," or whether he considers them collectively as a single "text."

37. On the subject of male protection of the female family members, see Dundes (1978, 258–59).

38. The centrality of the mother-son relationship in Middle Eastern society has been treated in detail by Dundes (1978, 288–89).

Chapter 6

1. For an in-depth study of the poetic qualities, see Bar-Itzhak 1987; 1990.

2. The narratives are kept in the Israeli Folktale Archives. The importance of ethnic categories was exhaustively discussed by Ben-Amos (1975; 1976), and I wanted to find out whether an ethnic category existed in the tradition of Moroccan Jews. The storytellers were asked to term the stories according to their own ethnic terms.

3. The book *Shevah Haim* was first published in the 1940s without a date. Of its 116 stories, 28 are about Rabbi Haim Pinto, all others are about different Jewish Moroccan saintly figures (Ben-Ami 1975, 209).

Bibliography

Aarne, Antti, and Stith Thompson. 1961. *The Types of the Folktale: A Classification and Bibliography.* 2nd Revision. Helsinki: Suomalainen Tiedeakatemia.

Alendaf, Avraham. 1928. *A Booklet to the History of Rabbi Shalem Shabazi and Sharabi* [in Hebrew]. Jerusalem.

Alexander, Tamar. 1994. "The Cinderella Tale: The Dress of Moon, Stars, and Sun" [in Hebrew]. *Bikoret U'parshanut* 30:157–73.

Alexander, Tamar, and Dov Noy. 1989. *The Treasure of Our Fathers: Judeo-Spanish Tales* [in Hebrew]. Jerusalem: Misgav Jerushalayim.

Alexander-Frizer, Tamar. 1999. *The Beloved Friend-and-a-Half,* Studies in Sepharadic Folk-Literature [in Hebrew]. Jerusalem: Magnes.

Amir, Yehuda. 1990. "A Letter by Rabbi Israel Levy to Yemen: She'araim, 1936–1937" [in Hebrew]. *Thema* 1:63–72.

An-Ski, S. (Shlomo-Zanvil Rapaport). 1925. *Collected Works* [in Yiddish]. Vol. 15. Vilna/Warsaw/New York: Ferlag An-Ski.

Attias, Moshe. 1976. *The Golden Feather of the Wonder Bird.* Haifa: Israel Folktale Archives.

Ayali, Meir. 1995. "Anxiety about Cutting Down Fruit Trees in Rabbinic Literature" [in Hebrew]. *Ki'Revivim.* Tel Aviv: Hakibbutz Ha'meuhad. 374–80.

Bakhtin, Mikhail M. 1981. *The Dialogic Imagination.* Austin: University of Texas Press.

Bar-Gal, Yoram, and Shmuel Shammai. 1983. "The Marshes of the Jezreel Valley: Legend and Reality" [in Hebrew]. *Cathedra* 72:163–79.

Bar-Itzhak, Haya. 1987. *"Saints' Legend" as Genre in Jewish Folk-Literature* [in Hebrew]. Unpublished PhD diss. Jerusalem: Hebrew University.

———. 1990. "Modes of Characterization in Religious Narrative: Jewish Folk Legends about Miracle Worker Rabbis." *Journal of Folklore Research* 27 (3):205–30.

———. 1992. "'And We Came to the Land of Our Forefathers . . .' The Folk Legend of Yemenite Jews in Israel." *Jewish Folklore and Ethnology Review* 14 (1–2):44–54.

———. 1993. "Jewish Moroccan Cinderella in Israeli Context." *Journal of Folklore Research* 30 (2–3):93–125.

———. 2001. *Jewish Poland: Legends of Origin, Ethnopoetics and Legendary*

Chronicles. Detroit: Wayne State University Press.

Bar-Itzhak, Haya, and Aliza Shenhar. 1993. *Jewish Moroccan Folk Narratives from Israel.* Detroit: Wayne State University Press.

———. 1993a. "Processes of Change in Israeli Society as Reflected in Folklore Research: The Beith-She'an Model" [in Hebrew]. *Jewish Folklore and Ethnology Review* 15:128–33.

Bascom, William R. 1953. "Folklore and Anthropology." *Journal of American Folklore* 66:283–90.

Bauman, Richard. 1986. *Story, Performance, and Event: Contextual Studies in Oral Narrative.* Cambridge: Cambridge University Press.

Ben-Ami, Isaschar. 1975. *Moroccan Jews: Ethno-cultural Studies* [in Hebrew]. Jerusalem: Rubin Mass.

Ben-Amos, Dan. 1971. "Toward a Definition of Folklore in Context." In *Toward New Perspectives in Folklore,* ed. A. Parades and R. Bauman. Austin: University of Texas Press. 3–15.

———. 1973. "The 'Myth' of Jewish Humor." *Western Folklore* 32:112–31.

———. 1975. "New Trends in Folklore Research" [in Hebrew]. *Ha'sifrut* 20: 1–8.

———. 1976. "Analytical Categories and Ethnic Genres." In *Folklore Genres,* ed. D. Ben-Amos. Austin: University of Texas Press, 215–42.

———. 1991. "Jewish Folklore Studies." *Modern Judaism* 11:17–66.

———. 1993. "Context in Context." *Western Folklore* 52:209–26.

Ben-Ari, Eyal, and Yoram Bilu. 1981. "Saints' Sanctuaries in Israeli Development Towns: On a Mechanism of Urban Transformation." *Urban Anthropology* 16 (2):243–71.

Ben-Ari, Nahum. 1936. *Ein Harod* [in Hebrew]. Tel Aviv: Amanut.

Ben-Raphael, Eliezer, et al. 1973. *A Study of the Kibbutz Leavers* [in Hebrew]. Haifa: Haifa University Press.

Bettelheim, Bruno. 1977. *The Uses of Enchantment: The Meaning and Importance of Fairy-tales.* New York: Vintage.

Bremond, Claude. 1970. "Morphology of the French Folktale." *Semiotica* 2: 247–76.

Bruner, Edward M., and Phyllis Gorfain. 1984. "Dialogic Narration and the Paradoxes of Masada." In *Text, Play, and Story: The Construction and Reconstruction of Self and Society,* ed. E. Bruner. Washington, DC: American Ethnological Society.

Brunwand, Jan Harold. 1968. *The Study of American Folklore: An Introduction.* New York: Norton.

Calame-Griaule, Geneviève. 1970. "Pour une etude ethnolinguistique des Litteratures orals africaines." *Langages* 5. Vol. 18: 22–47.

Cohen, Eitan. 2002. *The Moroccans: The Negative of the Ashkenazim.* Tel Aviv: Resling.

Cohen, Reuven. 1972. *The Kibbutz Settlement: Principles and Processes* [in Hebrew]. Tel Aviv: Ha'kibbutz Ha'meuchad.

Collins, John J. 1978. *Primitive Religion.* Totowa, NJ: Littlefield Adams.

Connerton, P. 1990. *How Societies Remember.* Cambridge: Cambridge University Press.

Cox, Marian Roalfe. 1893. *Cinderella.* London: Nutt.

Dafni, Amotz. 2004. "The Common Jujube: The Tree of the Seventh Heaven." Unpublished article.

Dan, Joseph. 1981. "The Beginnings of Hebrew Hagiographic Literature" [in Hebrew]. *Jerusalem Studies in Jewish Folklore* 1:82–100.

Dégh, Linda, and Andrew Vazsonyi. 1974. "The Memorat and the Proto Memorat." *Journal of American Folklore* 87:239–45.

Dolby Stahl, Sandra. 1989. *Literary Folkloristics and the Personal Narrative.* Bloomington: Indiana University Press.

Dorson, Richard M. 1972. "Legends and Tall Tales." In *Folklore: Selected Essays.* Bloomington: Indiana University Press. 159–72.

Dundes, Alan. 1968. Introduction to *Morphology of the Folktale,* by Vladimir Propp, 2nd edition. Austin: University of Texas Press. xi–xii.

———. 1978. "The Hero Pattern and the Life of Jesus." *Essays in Folkloristics.* Meerut, India: Folklore Institute. 223–62.

———, ed. 1982. *Cinderella: A Folklore Casebook.* New York: Garland.

———, ed. 1984. *Sacred Narrative: Readings in the Theory of Myth.* Berkeley: University of California Press.

Eberhard, Wolfram, and Pertev N. Boratav. 1953. *Typen Türkischer Volksmärchen,* Wiesbaden: F. Steiner.

Eisenstadt S. N. 1967. *Israeli Society.* Jerusalem: Magnes.

Elam, Keir. 1980. *The Semiotics of Theatre and Drama.* London: Methuen.

Eliade, Mircea. 1959. *Cosmos and History: The Myth of the Eternal Return.* Trans. Willard R. Trask. New York: Harper and Row.

———. 1968. *Myth and Reality.* New York: Harper and Row.

———. 1991. *The Myth of the Eternal Return or Cosmos and History.* Bollingen Series XLVI. Princeton, NJ: Princeton University Press.

Fine, Elizabeth C. 1984. *The Folklore Text: From Performance to Print.* Bloomington: Indiana University Press.

Frankenstein, K. 1951. "The Psychological Approach to the Problem of Ethnic Differences." *Magamot* 3(a): 158–70.

Gafner, Ya'acov Shalom. 1970. *Light of the Sun* [in Hebrew]. Jerusalem: Mifal Helkat Mehokek.

Gali, Gina. 1989. "Local Legends: The Kibbutz Folk Narrative" [in Hebrew]. *Alei-Siah* 26:243–50.

Geertz, Clifford. 1973. *The Interpretation of Cultures.* New York: Basic Books.

Georges, Robert A. 1983. "Folklore." In *Sound Archives: A Guide to Their Establishment and Development,* ed. David Lance. Milton Keynes, Eng.: International Association of Sound Archives.

———. 1983a. "Research Trends in Ethnic Folklore" [in Hebrew]. *Jerusalem Studies in Jewish Folklore* 4:7–26.

Gertz, Nurith. 1995. *Captive of a Dream, National Myths in Israeli Culture* [in Hebrew]. Tel Aviv: Am Oved.

Gilad, Lisa. 1989. *Ginger and Salt.* Boulder, CO: Westview.

Ginzberg, Levy. 1961. *Interpretation and Innovation in the Yerushalmi* [in Hebrew]. 4 vols. New York: Beit Midrash.

Goodman, Lenn E. 1993. "Mythic Discourse." In *Myth and Fiction,* ed. S. Biderman and B. A. Sharfstein. New York: Brill. 104–21.

Grimm, Jacob, and Wilhelm Grimm. 1960. *The Grimms' German Folktales.* Carbondale: Southern Illinois University Press.

Gutman, Yisrael. 1985. *The Jews in Poland after World War II* [in Hebrew]. Jerusalem: Zalman Shazar Center.

Ha'levi, Yehuda. 1984. *The Kuzari Book by Yehuda Ha'levi* [in Hebrew]. Tel-Aviv: Ha'menora.

Hasan-Rokem, Galit. 1982. "Processes of Change in the Folk Narrative" [in Hebrew]. *Jerusalem Studies in Jewish Folklore* 3:129–37.

———. 1988. "The Snake at the Wedding: A Semiotic Reconsideration of the Comparative Method of Folk Narrative Research." *ARV, Scandinavian Yearbook of Folklore* 43:73–87.

Honko, Lauri. 1964. "Memorates and the Study of Folk Belief." *Journal of the Folklore Institute.* 1–2, 5–19.

Hoze, Seadia. 1973. *The Book of the Life History of Rabbi Shalom Shabazi and the Customs of Shar'ab Jewry and the Book of Yemenite Exile* [in Hebrew]. Jerusalem: Kore Ha'dorot.

Jason, Heda. 1977. *Ethnopoetry: Form, Content, Function.* Bonn: Linguistica Biblica.

Kapach, Yoseph. 1961. *The Ways of Yemen: Jewish Life in San'a and Vicinity* [in Hebrew]. Jerusalem: Ben-Zvi Institute.

Katriel, Tamar. 1993. "Remaking Place: Cultural Production in an Israeli Pioneer Settlement Museum." *History & Memory* 5 (2):104–35.

Katriel, Tamar, and Aliza Shenhar. 1990. "Tower and Stockade: Dialogic Narration in Israeli Settlement Ethos." *Quarterly Journal of Speech* 76 (4):359–74.

Katz, Shaul. 1982. "The First Furrow: Ideology, Settlement, and Agriculture in Petah Tikva during its First Ten Years" [in Hebrew]. *Cathedra* 23:57–124.

Kipnis, Baruch. 1983. "The Development of the Jewish Settlement in the Galilee, 1948–1980" [in Hebrew]. In *The Lands of Galilee,* ed. A. Shmueli, A. Sofer, and N. Kliot. Haifa: Society for Applied Social Research, University of Haifa.

Kirk, G. S. 1970. *Myth: Its Meaning and Functions in Ancient and Other Cultures.* Berkeley: University of California Press.

Kirshenblatt-Gimblett, Barbara. 1975. "The Parable in Context." In *Folklore: Performance and Communication,* ed. Dan Ben-Amos and Kenneth Goldstein. The Hague: Mouton. 106–30.

————. 1978. "Culture Shock and Narrative Creativity." In *Folklore in the Modern World*, ed. Richard M. Dorson. The Hague: Mouton. 109–21.

————. 1983. "Studying Immigrant and Ethnic Folklore." In *Handbook of American Folklore*, ed. Richard M. Dorson. Bloomington: Indiana University Press. 39–47.

Klymasz, Robert Bogdan. 1980. *Ukrainian Folklore in Canada: An Immigrant Complex in Transition*. New York: Arno.

Knaani, David. 1986. *The Kibbutz in Hebrew Narratives* [in Hebrew]. Tel Aviv: Sifriat Poalim.

Kolakowski, Leszek. 1989. *The Presence of Myth*. Chicago: University of Chicago Press.

Lawson, Merlin P., and Charles W. Stockton. 1981. "Desert Myth and Climatic Reality." *Annals of the Association of American Geographers* 71:527–35.

Lévi-Strauss, Claude. 1963. "The Structural Study of Myth." In *Structural Anthropology*. New York: Basic Books. 206–31.

Lewis, Herbert S. 1989. *After the Eagles Landed: The Yemenites of Israel*. Boulder, CO: Westview.

Liebman, Charles, and Eliezer Don-Yehiya. 1983. *Civil Religion in Israel: Traditional Judaism and Political Culture in the Jewish State*. Berkeley: University of California Press.

Mabberley, D. J. 1981. *The Plant-Book: A Portable Dictionary of Higher Plants*. New York: Cambridge University Press.

Manoah, Yehoushua. 1971. "The Holiday of Planting Trees in the Jordan Valley" [in Hebrew]. *The Book of Holidays* 5, ed. Yom-Tov Levinsky. Tel Aviv: Oneg Shabat. 478–79.

Meir, Ofra. 1977. *The Acting Characters in the Stories of the Talmud and the Midrash* [in Hebrew]. Unpublished PhD diss. Jerusalem: Hebrew University.

Meron, Stanley. 1981. Introduction to *Kibbutz Makom: Report from an Israeli Kibbutz*, by Amia Lieblich. New York: Pantheon.

Mills, Margaret A. 1982. "A Cinderella Variant in the Context of Muslim Women's Ritual." In *Cinderella, A Folklore Casebook*, ed. Alan Dundes. New York: Garland. 185–89.

Muhawi, Ibrahim, and Sharif Kanaana. 1988. *Speak, Bird, Speak Again: Palestinian Arab Folktales*. Berkeley: University of California Press.

Nacht, Jacob. 1959. *The Symbols of Women in Ancient Hebrew Literature, Modern Hebrew Literature, and World Literature* [in Hebrew]. Tel Aviv: published by his students.

Noy, Dov. 1962. "Is There a Jewish Folk Joke?" [in Hebrew]. *Mahanayim* 67: 49–56.

————. 1967. "Rabbi Shalem Shabazi in the Folk Legend of Yemenite Jews" [in Hebrew]. In *Come Yemen*, ed. Y. Razhabi. Tel Aviv: Afikim. 106–31.

————. 1977. "The Death of Rabbi Shalem Shabazi in the Folk Legend of Yemenite Jews" [in Hebrew]. In *The Heritage of Yemenite Jewry: Studies and*

Research. Jerusalem: Bo'i Teiman, 132–49.

————. 1981. "Between Israel and Other Nations in the Folk Legend of Yemenite Jews" [in Hebrew]. In *Studies of Edot and Gniza.* Jerusalem: Magnes. 229–95.

Oring, Elliott. 1992. *Jokes and Their Relations.* Lexington: University Press of Kentucky.

Ortner, Sherry B. 1973. "On Key Symbols." *American Anthropologist* 75:1338–46.

Pace, David. 1982. "Beyond Morphology: Levi-Strauss and the Analysis of Folktales." In *Cinderella, A Folklore Casebook,* ed. Alan Dundes. New York: Garland. 245–58.

Parry, Milman, and Albert Bates Lord. 1953–1954. *Serbocroatian Heroic Songs,* 1–2. Cambridge: Harvard University Press.

Patai, Raphael. 1942. *Man and Soil* [in Hebrew]. Jerusalem: Hebrew University.

Pepper, Stephen. 1942. *World Hypothesis.* Berkeley: University of California Press.

Perrault, Charles. 1961. *Histoires ou contes du temps passè, avec de Moralites.* Paris.

Propp, Vladimir. 1968. *Morphology of the Folktale.* Austin: University of Texas Press.

————. 1971. "Generic Structures in the Russian Folklore." *Genre* 4:213–48.

Rabinowitz, Dan. 1996. *Overlooking Nazareth: The Ethnography of Exclusion in Galilee.* Cambridge: Cambridge University Press.

Raglan, Lord. 1956. *The Hero: A Study in Tradition, Myth, and Drama.* New York: Vintage.

Ramanujan, A. K. 1982. "Hanchi: A Kannada Cinderella." In *Cinderella, A Folklore Casebook,* ed. Alan Dundes. New York: Garland. 259–75.

Rank, Otto. 1959. *The Myth of the Birth of the Hero.* New York: Vintage.

Rooth, Anna Brigitta. 1951. *The Cinderella Cycle.* Lund: Gleerup.

Rosenberg, B. A. 1978. "The Genres of Oral Narratives." In *Theories of Literary Genre,* ed. Joseph P. Strelka. University Park: Pennsylvania State University Press. 150–65.

Rouget, Gilbert. 1966. "African Traditional Non-Prose Forms: Reciting, Declaiming, Singing and Strophic Structures." *Proceedings of Conference on African Languages and Literature.* Evanston, IL: Northwestern University Press.

Schely-Newman, Esther. 1991. *Self and Community in Historical Narratives: Tunisian Immigrants in an Israeli Moshav,* Unpublished diss. Chicago: University of Chicago.

Seri, Rachel. 1968. *The Holy Amulet* [in Hebrew]. Israel Folktale Archives Publication Series. Haifa: Israel Folktale Archives.

Shenhar, Aliza. 1989. "Legendary Rumors as Social Control in the Israeli Kibbutz." *Fabula* 30:63–82.

Sheub, H. 1970. "The Technique of the Expansible Image in Xhosa Ntsomi Performances." *Research in African Literature* 1:119–46.

Shoham, S. Giora, and Giora Rahav. 1967. "Social Stigma and Prostitution." *Annales Internationales de Criminologie* 6:479–513.

Shokeid, Moshe. 1987. "The Influence of the Aliya on the Jewish Moroccan Family in Israel" [in Hebrew]. *Hevra U'Revaha* 8:1, 3–14.

Shokeid, Moshe, and Shlomo Deshen. 1999. *The Generation of Transition: Continuity and Change among North-African Immigrants in Israel* [in Hebrew]. Jerusalem: Yad Yitzhak Ben Zvi.

Shtal, Avraham. 1970. "The Change of the Folk Narrative of Oriental Jews after Their Immigration" [in Hebrew]. *The Studies of the Center for Folklore Research* 1:313–37.

———. 1979. *Cultural Integration in Israel* [in Hebrew]. Tel Aviv: Am Oved.

Shur, Shimon. 1972. *Kibbutz Bibliography* [in Hebrew]. Tel Aviv: Higher Education and Research Authority of Federation of Kibbutz Movements.

Sivan, Emmanuel. 1991. *The 1948 Generation: Myth, Profile, and Memory* [in Hebrew]. Tel Aviv: Ma'arahot.

Smooha, Sammy. 1978. *Israel: Pluralism and Conflict.* Berkeley: University of California Press.

Sorski, Aharon. 1974. *Orient Lights* [in Hebrew]. Bnei-Brak.

Spiegel, G. 1963. "Ethnic Group Integration with Silk Gloves" [in Hebrew]. *Keshet* 5 (17):144–49.

Stark, R. 1965. "A Taxonomy of Religious Experience." *Journal for the Scientific Study of Religion* 5:97–116.

Strabo. 1932. *The Geography of Strabo.* Vol. 8, ed. and trans. Horace L. Jones. Loeb Classical Library. London: Heinemann.

Streng, Frederick J. 1969. *Understanding Religious Man.* Belmont, CA: Dickenson.

Tobi, Yoseph. 1972. *Shalom Ben-Yoseph Shabazi* [in Hebrew]. Jerusalem: General Community of Yemenite Jews in Jerusalem.

Tsoref, Avshalom. 1964. *Yisrael Levi of Gennosar* [in Hebrew]. Tel Aviv: Bitui.

Tylor, E. B. 1871. *Primitive Culture.* London: John Murray.

Waley, Arthur. 1947. "Earliest Chinese Cinderella Story." *Folk-Lore* 58.

Watson, J. W. 1971. "Geography and Image Regions." *Geographia Helvetica* 26:65–77.

Weil, S. 1983. "The Effect of Ethnic Origin on Children's Perception of Their Families." *Journal of Comparative Family Studies* 14:347–66.

Weinreich, B. S. 1960. "The Americanization of Passover." In *Studies in Biblical and Jewish Folklore,* ed. R. Patai, F. L. Utley, and D. Noy. Bloomington: Indiana University Press. 329–66.

Wilson, William A. 1989. "Herder, Folklore and Romantic Nationalism." In *Folk Groups and Folklore Genres,* ed. E. Oring. Logan: Utah State University Press.

Yanai, Aharon. 1971. *The History of Ein Harod* [in Hebrew]. Tel Aviv: Ha'kibbutz

Ha'meuhad.

Yassif, Eli. 1994. *The Hebrew Folktale: History, Genre, Meaning* [in Hebrew]. Jerusalem: Mosad Bialik.

Zerubavel, Yael. 1991. "New Beginning, Old Past: The Collective Memory of Pioneering in Israeli Culture." In *New Perspectives in Israeli History: The Early Years of the State,* ed. L. J. Silberstein. New York: New York University Press. 193–215.

Index of Names and Places

Aarne, Antti, 84, 118, 136, 137, 139, 141, 143
Aarne and Thompson (AT), 118, 143, 174, 175
Abas, Moshe, 17, 168
Abraham, 34, 35
Abu-Shusha, 21
Achihud, 97
Aden, 77, 86, 88
Afghanistan, 174
Africa, 10, 54, 59, 66, 67, 89, 90, 93–95, 97, 138, 154–57, 170,
Africa, North, 59, 66, 67, 89, 90, 93–95, 97, 156, 157, 170
Afula, 61
Akiva, Rabbi, 163
Alendaf, Avraham, 171
Alexander-Frizer, Tamar, 94, 173, 174
Algeria, 59
Allon, Yigal, 22, 25
Alterman, Natan, 35
Alzara Arpood, Esther, 174
America, 20, 53, 57
America, North, 57
Amichai, Yehuda, 35
Amir, Yehuda, 80, 85
Anders, Władysław, 66
An-Ski, S., 59
Arab Kingdoms, 76, 77
Aschenputtel, 139, 175
Ashdot Ya'akov, 11, 12
Ashkenazi, Ashkenazim, 54, 55, 60, 83, 85, 86
Ashqelon, 157
Asia, Asian, 54, 59, 93, 94 138, 156, 170
Atlas Mountains, 119
Attias, Moshe, 173
Avigdor from Migdal, 18

Ayali, Meir, 168

Ba'al Priests, 77
Bakhtin, Mikhail M., 10, 28
Balfour Declaration, ix, 3
Bar-Gal, Yoram, 13, 14, 167
Bar-Itzhak, Haya, 8, 54, 59, 60, 72, 73, 75, 94, 98, 101, 144, 170–73, 175
Bascom, William R., 53
Bashari, Shalom, 83, 86, 172
Basile, Giambattiste, 137, 138, 141
Bates Lord, Albert, 154
Bauman, Richard, 119
Beit-Ya'acov, Shlomo, 172
Ben-Ami, Issachar, 175
Ben-Ami, Mazal, 172
Ben-Amos, Dan, 5, 9, 53, 154, 168, 171, 175
Ben-Ari, Eyal, xi, 89, 90, 156
Benari, Nahum, 41
Benari, Yair, 30, 32, 36, 39–41, 43, 46, 47, 169
Ben-Gurion, David, 54, 171
Ben-Raphael, Eliezer, 49
Ben-Shemen, 7
Bettelheim, Bruno, 137, 138, 174
Bilu, Yoram, xi, 89, 90, 156
Boratav, Pertev N., 118
British, 8, 53
Bruner, Edward M., 10, 27, 28
Bukhara, 174

Calame-Griaule, Genevieve, 154
Canada, 172, 181
Carmel, Mount, 76, 77
Carmi, Moshe, 38, 169
Cinderella, 136–38, 141–44, 149, 150, 174, 175

185

Cinderella, American, 144
Cinderella, Moroccan. *See* Smeda Rmeda
Collins, John J., 156
Connerton, Paul, 48
Cox, Marian Roalfe, 136, 140, 174

Dafni, Amotz, 168
Dan, Joseph, 72, 155
Danino, Moshe, 157–59
Dayan, Haviva, 98–101, 116, 118, 119, 173
Deganya, 4, 8, 16
Dègh, Linda, 172
Diaspora, 16, 34, 40, 54, 55, 59, 60, 65, 71, 93
Dolby-Stahl, Sandra, 172
Don-Yehiya, Eliezer, 54, 65
Dorson, Richard M., 9, 71
Dundes, Alan, 117, 136, 144, 167, 174, 175
Duzzy, Rachel, 168

Eberhard, Wolfram, 118
Edot, Journal, ix
Egyptian, 140
Ein Harod, 8, 29–34, 36–49, 169
Ein Harod Me'uhad, 39
Ein Harod Yihud, 39
Eisenstadt, S.N., 4, 59, 65
Elam, Keir, 154
Eliade, Mircea, 36, 61, 72, 156
Elijah the Prophet (Tishbite), 67, 73, 76–79
England, 53
Eretz Israel. *See* Israel, Land of
Erez, Sara, 172
Ethiopia, 68, 93, 97, 172
Europe, 3, 14, 53, 59, 62, 67, 93, 140
Europe, Eastern, 57, 62, 93, 172
Ezekiel, 22

Fine, Elizabeth C., 173
Frankenstein, K., 54

Gafner, Ya'acov Shalom, 171
Gali, Gina, 5
Galilee, 7, 8, 16, 58, 97, 170
Galilee, Lower, 16, 58
Galilee, Sea of, 7, 8
Gedud Ha'avodah, 30, 43, 44

Geertz, Clifford, 153
Gellerman, Nahman, 43–45, 48
Gennosar, 7–13, 15, 16, 18, 19, 21–23, 25–28, 167, 168
Gennosar Valley, 8, 10
Georges, Robert A., 53, 54, 170
Germany, 3
Gertz, Nurith, ix
Gilad, Lisa, 172
Gilboa, Mount, 33–35
Ginzberg, Levy, 155
Givat Brenner, 8
Goldberg, Ya'akov, 171
Goldman, Yosef, 171
Gomułka, Władysław, 57
Goodman, Lenn, E., 9
Gorfain, Phyllis, 10, 27, 28
Gouri, Haim, 35
Greece, 118, 173
Grimm, Brothers, 139, 141, 175
Gutman, Yisrael, 57

Ha'levi, Yehuda, 164
Ha'Shomer Ha'Tsair, 43
Hadad, Batia, 172
Hafutah, Freha, 119, 120, 135, 136, 145, 146, 150
Haganah, 169
Haifa, 61, 97, 171
Halama, 112–15, 173
Hanina, Rabbi, 15
Haramauth, 171
Hartuv, 99
Hasan-Rokem, Galit, x, 54, 94, 171, 175
Hehalutz Movement, 3
Herder, Johann Gottfried von, 53
Hibba, Nissim, 172
Hillel, 33–35, 38
Hirsch, Baron Maurice de, 8
Honko, Lauri, 172
Hoze, Seadia, 171
Hungary, 58, 67

Imam Ahmed Iben Hassan Iben Alkassem, 171
Indian, 142
Iraq, 174
Israel, 1, 3–5, 7, 8, 10, 13–16, 26–28, 30,

32, 34–38, 45, 54, 55, 57–60, 63–66,
  68, 69, 71–74, 76–82, 84–91, 93–95,
  97–100, 116, 118–20, 135, 151, 153,
  156, 157, 161, 165, 167, 169–74
Israel Defense Forces, 32
Israel Folktale Archives (IFA), xi, 17, 23–
  25, 33, 37, 40, 44, 46, 55, 84, 85, 89,
  93, 98, 100, 102, 116, 118, 120, 137,
  139, 158, 161, 164, 167, 168, 171–74
Israel, Land of, ix, 1, 3, 4, 8, 13, 14, 16,
  26–28, 34–38, 72, 73, 76–79, 86–89,
  118, 167, 169, 172
Israel, State of, 3, 72, 77, 167

Jaffa, 80, 89, 157
Jason, Heda, 71
Jerusalem, 88
Jewish Agency, 8, 60–62
Jewish Colonization Association (ICA), 8
Jordan Valley, 16

Kanaana, Sharif, 168
Kaniuk, Yoram, 39
Kapach, Yoseph, 172
Kaplan, Noa, 18, 26, 27, 168
Katriel, Tamar, ix, 7, 14, 15, 20
Katz, Shaul, 14
Kenan, Amos, 30
Kfar Darom, 33
Kielce, 58
Kimchi, Billy, 174
Kinneret. *See* Galilee, Sea of
Kipnis, Baruch, 170
Kirk, G. S., 33
Kirshenblatt-Gimblett, Barbara, x, 57, 80,
  136, 172
Kiruani, Yosef Haim, 172
Klymasz, Robert Bogdan, 170
Knaani, David, 41
Kolakowski, Leszek, 38
Kritz, Iris, 168
Kurdistan, Iraqi, 174
Kurdistan, Persian, 174

Labor Brigade, 30, 169
Lamdan, Yitshak, 35
Laor, Yitshak, 35
Lavie, Shlomo, 30, 32–35, 169

Lawson, Merlin P., 167
Lebanon, Lebanese, 25, 97, 174
Lévi-Strauss, Claude, 61, 144, 175
Levy, Rabbi Israel, 80
Levy, Yisrael, 11, 13, 18, 21, 167
Lewis, Herbert, S., 172
Libya, 118, 173
Liebman, Charles, 54, 65
Lupan, Benny, 168
Lupan, Shulke, 18, 168
Lupan, Yovi, 18, 168

Ma'alot, 174
Mabberley, D. J., 167
Maghreb, 148
Majdal, 25
Makhluf Tarim, Mazal, 160
Maletz, David, 36, 37
Maletz, Rafi, 36
Malka, Mordekhai, 161
Malka, Nissim, 157
Manoah, Yehoshua, 16
Mapai Party, 63
Marii, Jamil, 16, 25, 26
Marrakesh, 125, 126
Massua, 99
Mediterranean, 118
Meir, Ofra, 156
Memphis, 140
Meron, Stanley, 48
Messiah, 34, 76, 77
Middle Eastern, 95, 148, 175
Migdal, 8, 17, 18, 21, 25
Mills, Margaret A., 174
Moriah, 34
Morocco, xi, 59, 67, 89, 95–101, 116, 117,
  119, 135, 137–44, 147, 150, 151, 153,
  155–57, 159, 165, 171, 173–75
Morri Salem. *See* Shabazi
Mother Alaguz, 99, 102–14, 116–19, 173
Muhammad, 25
Muhawi, Ibrahim, 168
Muslim countries, 84
Muz'a, 171

Nacht, Jacob, 140
Nahariya, 97
Natanya, 83, 84, 86, 88–90

Naukratis, 140
Nazareth, 58, 59, 65
Nazareth, Upper (Natzrat Illit), 58, 59, 64, 65, 67, 170, 171
Noam, 99
Noar Haoved, 8
Noy, Dov, 55, 59, 62, 73, 81, 171–73

Ofaqim, 157
Oring, Elliott, 62
Ortner, Sherry B., 28, 35, 38, 168

Pace, David, 144, 175
Palestine, ix, 3, 7, 8, 14, 169
Palestine Jewish Colonization Association (PICA), 8, 16, 25, 167
Palmach, 13, 169
Parry, Milman, 154
Patai, Raphael, 168
Pentamerone, Il, 137
Pepper, Stephen, 35
Perrault, Charles, 141, 143
Petah Tikva, 14
Pinto, Rabbi Haim, 164, 175
Poland, x, 57–65, 67
Polish Jews, x, 57, 59, 60, 64, 65, 68, 69, 170
Propp, Vladimir, 60, 154, 170

Qiryat Nazereth. *See* Nazareth, Upper

Rabinowitz, Dan, 170, 171
Raglan, Lord, 117
Rahav, Giora, 95
Ramanujan, A. K., 142
Rank, Otto, 117
Red Sea, 171
Reichenstein, Yoseph, 45
Rivner, Tuvia, 35
Ro'er, 21
Rodophis, 140
Romania, 3, 58, 67
Rooth, Anna Birgitta, 136, 174
Rosenberg, Bruce A., 153
Rothschild, Baron Edmond de, 8, 167
Rouget, Gilbert, 154
Russia, 3

S'hayek, Ovadia, 22, 25
Sambation River, 75
Samsam ben Kamkam, 139, 174
Samsam-Kamkam, 127, 139, 174
Sarah, 157, 158
Schely-Newman, Esther, x, 54
Scotland, 141
Sefad, 157
Sephardi, Sephardic, Sephardim, 55, 94, 118, 174
Seri, Yona, 172
Shabazi, Rabbi Shalom, 72–75, 83, 86–90, 171, 172
Sham'a, 75
Shammai, Shmuel, 13, 14, 167
Sharabi, Rabbi Shalom, 72, 73, 80–82, 89, 171
Shelomi, 97–99, 101, 165, 173
Shenhar, Aliza, ix, 5, 7, 15, 54, 94, 98, 101, 171, 173
Sheub, Harold, 153
Shevat, 16
Shlonski, Abraham, 35
Shmuel, Rabbi, 84
Shoham, S. Giora, 95
Shokeid, Moshe, 96, 99, 100
Shomrat, 168
Shtal, Avraham, 95, 171
Shturman, Atara, 39, 40, 170
Shturman, Haim, 30, 39
Shur, Shimon, 5
Sicily, 118
Sivan, Emmanuel, 9, 38, 169, 170
Smeda Rmeda, 119–21, 134, 136–42, 144–50, 174, 175
Smoller, Hersh, 57
Smooha, Sammy, 55
Sobol, Yehoshua, 43
Sorski, Aharon, 171
Soviet Union, 93, 97, 172
Spanish, 167
Spiegel, G., 54, 55
Stark, Rodney, 156
Stockton, W., 167
Strabo, 140
Streng, Frederick J., 156
Sudan, 172

Syria, 25, 118

Ta'ez, 86, 87, 89, 171
Tabenkin, Yitshak, 30
Tel Aviv, 7
Tel Hai, ix, 9, 169, 170
Tel Yosef, 8
Thompson, Stith, 84, 118, 136, 137, 139, 141, 143
Tobi, Yoseph, 171
Trumpeldor, Joseph, ix, 47, 169, 170
Tsoref, Avshalom, 11
Tsoref, Yehudit, 167
Tunisia, 59, 174
Turkey, Turkish, 23, 118, 171, 173, 174
Tylor, Edward, 53

U'Moshe, Rabbi David, 157–59
United States, 167

Vazsonyi, Andrew, 172

Waley, Arthur, 174

Watson, J. W., 167
Weil, Shalva, 96
Weinreich, B. S., 170
Wilson, William A., 170
Wiseltier, Meir, 35
Yanai, Aharon, 30
Yassif, Eli, 156
Yehoshua, A. B., 35
Yemen, 71, 72, 74–77, 79, 81, 84, 85, 87–90, 97–171, 174
Yemenite Jews, x, 71, 76, 77, 79, 81, 82, 84–86, 89, 90, 171, 172
Yerubaal, 33, 35, 38
Yifat, 20
Yizhar, S., 35
Yugoslavia, 97, 118

Zand, Moniek, 171
Zerubavel, Yael, ix, 9, 47
Zezolla, 137
Zikhron Ya'akov, 45
Zisling, Aharon, 30

www.ingramcontent.com/pod-product-compliance
Lightning Source LLC
Chambersburg PA
CBHW070332270326
41926CB00017B/3850